Long-Term Financial Planning

Creative Strategies for Local Government

Long-Term Financial Planning:
Creative Strategies for Local Government

The International City Management Association is the professional and educational organization for chief appointed management executives in local government. The purposes of ICMA are to enhance the quality of local government and to nurture and assist professional local government administrators in the United States and other countries. In furtherance of its mission, ICMA develops and disseminates new approaches to management through training programs, information services, and publications.

Managers, carrying a wide range of titles, serve cities, towns, counties, and councils of governments in all parts of the United States and Canada. These managers serve at the direction of elected councils and governing boards. ICMA serves these managers and local governments through many programs that aim at improving the manager's professional competence and strengthening the quality of all local governments.

The International City Management Association was founded in 1914; adopted its City Management Code of Ethics in 1924; and established its Institute for Training in Municipal Administration in 1934. The Institute, in turn, provided the basis for the Municipal Management Series, generally termed the "ICMA Green Books."

ICMA's interests and activities include public management education; standards of ethics for members; the *Municipal Year Book* and other data services; urban research; and newsletters, a monthly magazine, *Public Management*, and other publications. ICMA's efforts for the improvement of local government management—as represented by this book—are offered for all local governments and educational institutions.

Long-Term Financial Planning

Creative Strategies for Local Government

Edited by
Jeffrey I. Chapman

ICMA

PRACTICAL MANAGEMENT SERIES
Barbara H. Moore, Editor

Long-Term Financial Planning
Capital Financing Strategies for Local Governments
Creative Personnel Practices
The Entrepreneur in Local Government
Human Services on a Limited Budget
Managing New Technologies
Microcomputers in Local Government
Police Management Today
Practical Financial Management
Productivity Improvement Techniques
Risk Management Today
Shaping the Local Economy
Successful Negotiating in Local Government
Telecommunications for Local Government

The Practical Management Series is devoted to the presentation of information and ideas from diverse sources. The views expressed in this book are those of the contributors and are not necessarily those of the International City Management Association.

Library of Congress Cataloging in Publication Data

Long-term financial planning.
  (Practical management series)
  Bibliography: p.
  Jeffrey I. II. International City Management
  1. Local finance—United States. I. Chapman,
Association. III. Series.
HJ275.L66 1987   352.1′0973   87-2613
ISBN 0-87326-076-7

Printed in the United States of America.
929190898887
54321

Foreword

To meet the financial pressures created by decreasing federal funds, tax and expenditure limitations, and other fiscal constraints, local governments have employed varied strategies—"cutback management," alternative service delivery mechanisms, user charges, impact fees, and creative financing techniques. Spurred by the need to do more with less, local governments may sometimes get caught up in the gimmicks and overlook the basics—in this case, sound forecasting, budgeting, and economic development strategies that can assure financial health over the long haul.

Long-Term Financial Planning: Creative Strategies for Local Government assumes that the finance function in local government has changed permanently—that finance directors, managers, and planners will be increasingly entrepreneurial, will make many decisions not in isolation but in the context of comprehensive economic and financial strategies, and will find themselves increasingly constrained by events outside their control. This book provides a foundation for intelligent long-term financial management, taking a look at what local governments can expect in the financial future; describing successful planning, budgeting, and forecasting techniques; and looking at a few potential revenue sources that are often overlooked.

This book is part of ICMA's Practical Management Series, which is devoted to serving local officials' needs for timely information on current issues and problems.

We are grateful to Jeffrey I. Chapman, Professor of Public Administration, University of Southern California, and Director, Sacramento Public Affairs Center, for organizing and compiling the volume. We also appreciate the cooperation of the organizations and individuals who granted ICMA permission to reprint their materials, and the work of the ICMA staff members who contributed to the effort. Thanks also go to David S. Arnold, who helped plan the entire Practical Management Series.

William H. Hansell, Jr.
Executive Director
International City
    Management Association

About the Editor

Jeffrey I. Chapman is a Professor of Public Administration at the University of Southern California and Director of the school's Sacramento Public Affairs Center. He has written extensively in the areas of state and local public finance, with particular emphasis on the interactions of land use controls, economic development, and the local public financial sector. He has also consulted with local and state governments and the national government on these topics. Professor Chapman received his A.B. degree from Occidental College and his M.A. and Ph.D. degrees in economics from the University of California at Berkeley.

About the Authors

Following are the affiliations of the contributors to *Long-Term Financial Planning* at the time of writing:

Roy Bahl, Professor of Economics and Public Administration, and Director, Metropolitan Studies Program, the Maxwell School, Syracuse University.

Bruce J. Bergman, Attorney, Roach and Bergman, Carle Place, New York.

Arlyne S. Bernhard, Systems Planning Consultant, Milwaukee, Wisconsin.

Richard Erickson, Correspondent, *American City & County* magazine, San Antonio, Texas.

John M. Kamensky, General Government Division, U.S. General Accounting Office.

M. Leanne Lachman, President and Chief Executive Officer, Real Estate Research Corporation, Chicago, Illinois.

Charles A. Lerable, Senior Urban Planner, City of Salinas, California.

Spyros Makridakis, European Institute of Business Administration.

Astrid E. Merget, George Washington University, Washington, D.C.

John E. Petersen, Director, Government Finance Research Center, Government Finance Officers Association, Washington, D.C.

Douglas D. Peterson, Senior Policy Analyst, National League of Cities, Washington, D.C.

Paul L. Pryde, Jr., Co-Founder, Pryde, Roberts and Company, Washington, D.C.

Larry Schroeder, Professor of Public Administration and Economics, and Senior Research Associate, Metropolitan Studies Program, the Maxwell School, Syracuse University.

William Schweke, Vice President for Programs, Corporation for Enterprise Development, Washington, D.C.

John Toon, Manager for Research and Publications, Advanced Technology Development Center, Georgia Institute of Technology.

Martin Wachs, Professor of Urban Planning, University of California, Los Angeles, California.

Thomas E. Ward, Director of Development, Newport News, Virginia.

John W. Wetzler, Vice President, Capital Investment Bank, Citibank, N.A.

Steven C. Wheelwright, Harvard Business School, Harvard University.

George Whelan, Capital Program Director, City of Philadelphia, Pennsylvania.

Donald R. Winkler, Professor, School of Public Administration, University of Southern California, Los Angeles, California.

C. Kurt Zorn, Assistant Professor of Public and Environmental Affairs, Indiana University, Bloomington, Indiana.

Contents

PART 1

Directions for the Future

The Future of Local Government Finance

Jeffrey I. Chapman

While the financial future of local government seems complex and chaotic, it is possible to distill much of the chaos into three trends that dominate the local financial horizon. Although few in number, these trends are of such major importance that the finance function in the future will bear scant resemblance to the traditional function in local governments today. These trends affect all those involved in financial planning and decision making—local governing bodies, appointed managers and administrators, planners, and finance directors. Those who understand the trends and act accordingly will be successful; those who do not will put their cities and jobs in jeopardy.

Three trends in local government finance

In short, those involved in local government finance will become increasingly entrepreneurial, will make many of their decisions not in isolation but in the context of comprehensive economic and financial strategies, and will find themselves increasingly dependent on events occurring outside their spheres of influence and control.

Trend 1: An entrepreneurial outlook Those involved in local government management, planning, and finance are no longer solely administrators of their respective functional areas. Rather, they have become entrepreneurial in outlook and will continue to be so in the future.

Although the term *entrepreneur* has been used to justify the wheelings and dealings surrounding many shady projects and is rapidly becoming a cliché, it originally was a term of respect. It meant a person who was willing and eager to undertake new activities in which there were possibilities of success. It is in this sense that the term should be applied to local governments. The finance officer of the future, for example, will remain responsible for the conservative care and control of the public purse, but will also be forced to examine risks, analyze projects, generate new ideas, and stimulate economic growth.

While there have always been risks in government finance, the risks in the future will be different in both quality and quantity. The technical specialist, the finance officer, will need to be far more sensitive to such concerns as interest rate fluctuations and the options market, the roles of hedging and arbitrage, and the possibility that anticipated revenue and cost streams will not occur. Finance officers, managers, and planners will need to analyze new ideas and relationships—for example, the role of budgeting in economic development will need to be carefully thought through to prevent the local government from making ad hoc decisions based on fads rather than considered decisions based on economic and financial analysis. And, as economic growth becomes increasingly necessary to secure the local revenue base, these actors are likely to be key individuals in ensuring that this growth does occur. Without an entrepreneurial role, managers and planners become caretakers, and finance officers are simply high-priced accountants.

Trend 2: A strategic approach   While the annual budget has always reflected practical choices among different revenue sources and expenditure categories, in the future it will also reflect strategic choices. Budgets can be used to enhance or retard economic development, local planning, or choice of infrastructure. The budget format and time orientation can encourage decision makers to either plan for or ignore the future. The city or county manager and the finance director have a large say in the choice of format as well as in the choice of the time horizon.

Included within this broad trend is the responsibility of the finance officer for predicting revenues and expenditures. This also involves a choice of time horizon, both looking backward into the past (to determine where to start the trend line) and looking forward into the future (to determine how far the projection should go). Further, the specification of the appropriate forecasting function is often an artistic choice rather than a theoretical or empirical one. Yet, plans for all sorts of contingencies depend on forecasts. By control of the forecasting function, the finance officer is in a key position in the financial decision-making process. By conscious awareness of the possibilities of future events that can come from different ways of forecasting, those who make and use forecasts can make choices that reflect their best beliefs of the realities of the future. These choices will also reflect the strategies that are employed to reach this future.

Trend 3: Increasing interdependence Increased interdependence will occur in two areas. The first is in the political arena. In this case, financial decisions are both constrained and enhanced by priorities of various departments within the jurisdiction, by mandates and economic conditions within the United States, and by worldwide barriers and opportunities.

Within the jurisdiction, financial decisions are inseparable from such activities as land use planning and economic development. Within the country, local finances are affected by tax code changes, additional local service responsibilities, and changing inflation and employment rates. In the world community, the local officials will need to be responsive to possibilities for local investment and markets abroad for both goods and capital. Changes in any of these factors will affect the economic conditions of the jurisdiction and thus its projected revenues and expenditures.

Interdependence also will increase within the budget itself. On the revenue side, the multiplicity of modern revenue streams argues that actions taken to increase one type of revenue could affect the availability of other types. For example, increases in business taxes could result in business relocation and thus a decline in sales tax revenues. As revenue sources increase, the chances for interdependent movements also increase. The same arguments can be made regarding expenditures. As jurisdictions change the mix of services they provide and perhaps move toward increased use of the private sector, they may find unanticipated effects on expenditures. For example, by contracting out they may save direct labor costs but incur the same aggregate level of expenditures. As an aside, it should be noted that accurate decisions concerning revenue and expenditure trade-offs often rely on basic economic analysis concerning questions of tax incidence, marginal decision making, and opportunity costs.

Although these long-run trends have been discussed as if they are independent, they are not. An entrepreneur is also a strategizer, and all local activities take place in an increasingly interdependent environment. Successful managers will understand this future environment and take actions, both strategic and entrepreneurial, that will position the jurisdiction as favorably as possible. The purpose of this book is to show some specific effects of these trends and some innovative responses by local governments.

Overview of the book

This book is divided into five sections. The first is a general look at the future of local finance, including the future role of the municipal finance officer and the constraints imposed by external events. The second is concerned with techniques for stimulating economic growth for the long term. The third explicitly examines the budgetary strategies available for infrastructure, planning, and economic development, while the fourth discusses forecasting methods and problems. The last section identifies future techniques that clever finance officers will be able to use to raise revenues and implicitly indicates several of these revenue interdependencies. The trends identified earlier recur throughout these sections.

Directions for the future The selections in this section urge the finance officer and other financial decision makers to look beyond the current bounds of their offices and to be aware of emerging opportunities.

John Wetzler and John Petersen argue that future finance directors must organize the finance function around analysis and planning as well as the budgeting of public funds. They argue that with a "rolling readjustment" of a strategic plan based on capital costs, returns on investment, risk and return trade-offs, and financial flexibility, a finance officer can provide far better financial management. It is important to note that Wetzler and Petersen assume a broad definition of management as an underlying assumption of the finance officer's role.

Next, Douglas Peterson and Donald Winkler look at the Tax Reform Act of 1986, a striking example of the interdependency that affects a local government's financial position. They indicate that there will be a set of pervasive responses to the tax act—changes in the tax base, the tax rate, the choice of taxes, and the costs of services. They also note some of the intergovernmental fiscal effects that result from the capping of tax-exempt bonds. Important to their argument is the assumption that local financial planners understand basic economic principles and how these principles can affect the behavior of individuals.

Stimulating future economic growth The underlying assumptions in the next section are that for most jurisdictions orderly growth is necessary for economic survival and that to achieve it local officials need to be both entrepreneurs and strategists.

Richard Erickson's article on economic development trends emphasizes that local officials must go out and aggressively pursue ways of stimulating growth. Through a series of small case studies it illustrates the variety of ways that local communities can be both entrepreneurial and strategic planners as they attempt to attract new companies.

Consistent with this approach is the article by William Schweke urging local governments to adopt an entrepreneurial policy. He believes that without an aggressive outreach program to attract firms and develop new small businesses, local government will find that there will be an inadequate supply of jobs being created.

He notes the consistent evidence that more than half of all new jobs are created by small independent entrepreneurs. He argues that these small entrepreneurs are particularly dependent on and responsive to their local communities and that is why the local communities can be very important in attracting and nurturing successful entrepreneurs.

Next, John Toon discusses a specific case of economic growth management—business incubators. These special environments, which support new small businesses in their early and fragile years, are another tool local government can utilize to stimulate economic growth. These incubators can be associated with universities, cities and counties, and industry and are designed to combat the undercapitalization and poor business management that often hinder small firms. Some local governments have approached the business and university sectors of the jurisdiction, and the three have formed quasi-partnerships to help the new small businesses.

The next piece underscores the interdependence of the local and world economies. Thomas Ward argues that it is possible for local governments to engage in international trade to stimulate local economic development. He identifies several techniques that can be used to enter the global economy and urges communities to band together to promote international trade. Again, implicit in this suggestion is that local decision makers have the entrepreneurial and strategic outlook that will make them receptive to a series of projects that must be very new to the established way of doing business.

Paul Pryde looks at ways to fund economic development initiatives. Picking up on the interdependence trend, he notes that cutbacks in federal assistance are forcing local governments to find new ways to generate private investment for growth-inducing ventures. He identifies two new ways—recycling development loans and funding development deposits with pension assets—and explains how they can stimulate growth.

Following these articles, all of which advocate the aggressive pursuit of economic growth, Charles Lerable argues that care must be taken by local governments when they cost out the fiscal impact of that growth. In particular, it is easy to make mistakes in fiscal impact analysis and extreme care must be used if the results are to have meaning. Lerable's checklist of potential mistakes is quite valuable for evaluating economic development projects.

Budgeting strategies   The budgeting articles are heavily focused on strategic behavior, arguing that carefully thought out local government budget processes can affect economic growth, the construction and maintenance of infrastructure, and comprehensive local planning.

George Whelan examines the complex role of the finance officer with respect to economic development. Not only is the traditional role still applicable—the finance officer is still the guardian of the public purse—but numerous other responsibilities are now inherent in that role. The finance officer needs to analyze a variety of special situations, ranging from speculative projects to customized inducements. Whelan urges the finance officer to be aware of the many trade-offs between the fiscal position of the city and the activity the city must undertake to encourage development.

John Kamensky then notes that public infrastructure investment has fallen short of infrastructure needs (although he agrees that "needs" is a nebulous term). He believes that a budgeting strategy for infrastructure could be usefully implemented to help obtain the necessary investment. He advances a set of principles for infrastructure finance based on a clear definition of fiscal responsibility and incentives for reduced demand. He believes that these principles will help the local government provide infrastructure based on demonstrated demand, and thus a more efficient level of infrastructure will be provided.

Next is a case study in which Arlyne Bernhard and Leanne Lachman describe Milwaukee's budgeting system for coordinating the distribution of Community Development Block Grant funds with the city's comprehensive planning strategy. And, although CDBG monies are being reduced, the Milwaukee experience has applications that go beyond this specific example; it can be a model for integrating the financial system of a jurisdiction with the planning process—a linkage that is absolutely necessary but too often ignored.

Fiscal forecasting   A necessary component of any discussion of long-run financial management is multi-year forecasting. It is impossible to be an entrepreneur or a strategizer without knowing what is expected to occur under various future assumptions. When done well, long-run forecasting forces an explicit accounting of the interdependencies that affect the future fiscal state of the jurisdiction. The four articles in this section address these issues.

Steven Wheelwright and Spyros Makridakis look at the practical problems of organizing and implementing a forecasting unit in an organization. Although the article is addressed to the private, corporate sector, many of the concerns it raises are equally applicable to the public sector. And the solutions and techniques are equally relevant.

Roy Bahl and Larry Schroeder identify techniques that can be utilized in forecasting both expenditures and revenues. What is particularly useful in this article is the explicit linkage of forecasting to budget preparation. Case studies of several cities are included in the descriptions as illustrations of particular points.

For the technically inclined, Kurt Zorn next discusses one particular type of forecasting method in some detail—econometric forecasting of revenues. He delineates several steps that must be undertaken in the development of the forecasting model and then discusses problems inherent in such models. Of particular value are Zorn's recommendations for surmounting the problems and generating an accurate forecast.

Finally, and perhaps most important, Martin Wachs raises the issue of ethics in forecasting, especially when forecasts are used to adjust public policy. Wachs urges care in the interpretation and potential political use of forecasts, since he believes that many forecasts are statements of hope and advocacy. It is sometimes easy to lose sight of this when the forecasts revolve around budgetary numbers.

Future revenue sources

Finally, the book takes a brief look at future revenue sources for local governments. Volumes have been written, of course, on user charges, impact fees, revenue collection methods, and other potential sources. This section does not cover that same ground and is by no means intended to be all-inclusive. Rather, it highlights three separate areas in which revenue streams can be generated and is meant to stimulate thinking about future potentials.

Astrid Merget examines in depth potential revenues that could come from the service sector. She analyzes the tax base and tax instruments available for several service industries. Her conclusions are not optimistic—scrambling for future revenues from service industries may be counterproductive, and simply securing service firms as part of an economic development strategy is not likely to be helpful. She ultimately urges a strategy of greater revenue diversification and tax tailoring.

An analysis by the California Office of Planning and Research suggests the ways in which local governments that are under fiscal stress can finance the infrastructure necessary for economic development to occur. Although based on California jurisdictions and their responses to the fiscal stress in that state, the article is applicable beyond the state's borders. The political, legal, and philosophical quagmire of California required innovation, strategizing, and awareness of interdependencies that generated some sophisticated responses. These responses, especially for difficult-to-finance facilities, can be useful to innovative (and brave) financial planners elsewhere in the country.

Bruce Bergman then discusses a third way to raise money—

selling off public property, a method that is certain to receive increasing public attention. This is a pragmatic piece, based on the assumption that the decision to sell has already been made. It is designed as a checklist for public officials so that they can realize the maximum benefits from their decisions.

Together, the articles in this book cover a variety of topics, all of them illustrating the possibilities that can become realities in the future if financial managers and planners are creative, willing to make long-run decisions, and alert to the interdependence of local, national, and world economies. New ideas are always arising, and managers should always be on the lookout for new possibilities and chances for innovation. Hopefully this book provides a first step.

The Finance Officer as Public Strategist

John W. Wetzler and John E. Petersen

The world of the state treasurer and the city or county controller has changed dramatically, but the institution of the office itself has not kept pace. In an ideal world, how would one organize the finance function for government entities? Answering such a question does not deal with the world as it is, but as it could be. This article considers the evolving role of the chief financial officer in government, drawing heavily on the experience of their private-sector counterparts to look at how the job has been changing.

Examining job titles is a good way to define, or redefine, the finance officer's role. A job title provides shorthand insights into the job's functions, and a review of job titles in the government finance area provides clues about the diversity of the field and the surprising array of disciplines it encompasses. In addition to the titles finance director and treasurer, the following labels are attached to members of this profession: clerk, comptroller, accountant, fiscal officer, budget director, chief financial manager, director of management and budget, internal auditor, revenue administration manager, investment specialist, financial officer and fiscal analyst.

What do these titles mean? How have the roles and responsibilities of the public financial officer changed? What changes are expected—and required—in the future to make the finance function more efficient?

All of the above titles represent various aspects of the finance function which, more likely than not, are scattered throughout a government's organizational structure. What these titles mean and how the functions fit together are significant concerns, although the

Reprinted with permission from the April 1985 issue of *Government Finance Review.*

various responsibilities are in many cases predefined by constitution or statute. Nevertheless, the pace and direction of change can be delineated by looking at existing financial institutions and their objectives.

The structure of the finance function

The concept of the finance director is rooted in turn-of-the-century efforts toward "good government" which was thought to require a concentration of executive authority. The idea of concentrating financial responsibility resulted as a logical requirement for more business-like government. During the turn of the century, fragmented local governments were immersed in an atmosphere of corruption, as city treasuries were systematically looted by plundering political machines, and public payrolls were padded without regard to tests of fitness or merit. Faced with an entrenched spoils system, reformers fought to concentrate administrative authority in chief executives as the best means of ensuring responsible government. They also thought, as a practical matter, that the financial aspects of administration must be concentrated in the hands of an officer reporting to a chief executive. And there was an awareness of the need to upgrade the profession, especially the aspects of financial reporting and accounting.

Seizing on the concept that finance cuts across all programs, the reform architects expected the newly fashioned directors to extend the advantage of their position to: (1) enforce municipal policies by means of finance-related controls; (2) represent and enforce the values of economy and efficiency throughout the organization; and (3) provide broad policy advice on the financial consequences of issues facing the government. Thus, the twin responsibilities of coordination and control were the central values of the new centralized finance function.

It is clear that in the future finance directors must be concerned with much more than care of and control over the public purse. The future of municipal government depends on the finance director's ability to invest the office with analytical and planning values. Simply because governments provide public services that generate *political* dividends, rather than monetary profits, this must not obscure their importance as representatives of very large financial enterprises. Serious efforts to organize the finance function around analytical and planning activities might have profound effects on current organizational and procedural arrangements, to say nothing of politics. But these changes must come about if the finance function is to be used effectively in government.

What is strategic planning?

Strategic planning is a process, an orderly way of looking at an organization's position in its environment. It is a type of analytical thinking that seeks to make explicit the overall missions and goals of an organization as they affect and are affected by the organization's environment. It emphasizes data gathering and analysis as ways to examine the array of external and internal factors that affect an organization's functioning. In the ideal case, strategic thinking, or strategic managing, is action oriented and looks to the future. "Vision," "game plan" and "issues management" are terms (buzz words) frequently voiced in the strategic planning vernacular.

Private firms have employed strategic planning as an integral part of their corporate operations for more than 20 years. The process is now highly developed in the corporate world, though planners are quick to point out that it is far from perfect. Many corporations have institutionalized it into high-level positions with titles such as corporate strategic planner, strategic manager and manager/future research. Strategic planning is now beginning to make a name for itself among government managers as public officials more and more frequently consider themselves business persons.

Frankly, all is not well with the performance of strategic planning as practiced by corporate America. But the problems with strategic planning have to do more with the difficulties in the application of the concept rather than with the idea itself. An article in *Business Week* magazine pointed to several corporations that have pioneered the strategic planning concept and committed either one or both of two sins. Either they had allowed the planning process to be divorced from the day-to-day management process (hence, it lost its relevance and sensitivity to the environment) or they had encumbered the process with so many forms and number-crunching exercises so as to freeze the process itself (hence, it lost its bias for action). The lesson here is that strategic planning really must be thought of as strategic management. For it to be effective, strategic planning must be conducted at levels where there is contact with and sensitivity to the changing environment. In addition, it must be flexible when carrying out plans so that the process supports effective operations and does not stymie and bog them down with endless paper exercises.

Among public managers, strategic management may seem to be just another name for organized common sense—just what innovative public officials have been doing for years. However, strategic management principles have not been institutionalized into a process that regularly is used to support decisionmaking at the highest levels of government. In the state and local government finance area, there have been trends in budgeting and organizational structures that reflect many of the important concepts of strategic planning. The progression from line-item budgets, to management by objectives and program budgets, and then to zero-based budgeting suggests an evolution toward strategic financial management. Indeed, the term "strategic budgeting" has become part of today's literature. In the sense of financial activities, strategic planning requires that finance managers develop a decisionmaking framework, identify specific goals and objectives (not just for the finance office, but for the whole community), establish priorities and implement the component activities necessary to achieve them.

The following presents, in fairly general terms, a model for strategic financial planning that has its roots in the private sector. The discussion focuses on four basic concepts and proceeds to the dynamics of the process itself.

The concept of strategic financial planning

Strategic financial planning is based on four concepts: capital costs, return on investment, risk and return trade-offs and financial flexibility. This is not to suggest that this is the only way to slice the pie, rather, it is a good general description. These concepts, while initially set forth in the private sector, can be applied to the public sector.

Capital costs   Governments require financial capital to operate. The employment of capital places monetary costs on governments (and taxpayers and ratepayers) who must either pay to raise money in the capital markets or forgo interest earnings if they use internally generated funds to finance their own operations and physical investments.

Return on investment   Just as capital has a cost, its efficient employment requires that it earn its keep by generating returns. In the case of capital that is invested in financial assets, such returns are directly measurable in the form of interest, dividends and capital gains and losses. When capital is dedicated to physical improvements or to support operations, measurement of its returns is more subjective and must be imputed in most cases. This is especially true for governmental activities where there is no bottom line in terms of profit or loss. Still, the concept holds that use of capital among competing needs must be justifiable as earning the required economic or social return. This is clearly the area least subject to measurement, but return on investment is implicit in every expenditure decision made in the public sector.

Risk and return trade-offs   The financial markets traditionally have made risk adjustments to compensate for the greater risks inherent in some types of investments as opposed to others. Essentially, this means that the anticipated return on a riskier investment needs to exceed that on an investment that is less risky, and the ultimate economic returns on various uses of capital are assessed in terms of the risks that have been assumed in financing the activity. The concept is valid in governments where the allocation of funds into one use may mean a higher likelihood that the benefits will not be enjoyed or future revenues received. The credit rating differential on various types of municipal bonds is evidence of the sensitivity of the credit markets to varying elements of risk.

Financial flexibility   Financial planning must take into consideration the ability of a unit to adjust its mix of capital resources and their allocation at any given time. This concept is especially important when assessing the ability of the unit to absorb risk. In some cases, this may appear to be a limited possibility for many governments until one reasons that the prospect of dependable future earnings or the strength of a proven revenue stream can constitute part of that resource base, and that changes in the mix that will take place over time are of value at any given point in time.

Steps in the strategic financial planning process

The key to strategic planning is that it identifies basic goals and objectives and then develops a series of action steps to implement them. The strategic plan is dynamic in the sense that the objectives are reshaped in anticipation of, or in response to, changing conditions. Implementation, therefore, is always accomplished by a "rolling readjustment" and a periodic re-evaluation of the plan itself. This is the dynamic versus the static model mentioned earlier.

In actual practice, the process of strategic planning is seldom sequential, having one step follow neatly after another. However, the following major decision blocks should help structure the types of considerations that enter into the planning process: examining the environment; assessing the current situation; setting goals and recognizing constraints; and identifying the alternatives.

Examining the environment   Essentially, this means that the government contemplating the provision of a service or making an improvement to its facilities must examine factors that are external and largely beyond its control. It must analyze things such as, where is the relevant technology heading, what regulatory trends are evident, what are the potential developments in the local economy and what is the political situation? This process is akin to the market study often undertaken by industry when it contemplates introducing a new product or changing its production process.

Assessing the current situation   This phase of plan development is more of an internally oriented perspective, and basically involves weighing objectively the government's existing financial condition, its operating performance, its technological and managerial capacity in relation to the demands made upon them and the political relationships. In many ways, this assessment sets the stage for setting goals and responding to changing conditions, at least in the short run. It also helps identify those factors over which a government has immediate control, such as its internal organization and the deployment of existing resources, as opposed to those environmental factors, such as the condition of the local and national economies, over which it can exercise little, if any, influence.

Setting goals   Goal setting is a consequence of the above exercises in which the external and internal factors have been taken fully into account in arriving at a realistic assessment of the situation. The goals, while general in the sense of defining strategies, need to be articulated in the form of acceptable ranges of values and trade-offs among outcomes. They also need to be explicit in observing what will be the relevant time, legal and economic constraints. For example, a goal such as supplying a particular government service to the greatest number of people at the lowest possible cost is so vague as to constitute no guide at all. Rather, goals need to concentrate on things such as specifying acceptable minimums of service, maximums of costs, levels of financial risk and priorities among competing groups of needs over time. In short, the goals need to concentrate on the allocation of resources—the basic job of an elected official in a democratic government.

Identifying the alternatives   Having assessed the external and internal factors that influence the setting of goals, and then specifying those goals—the three previous steps—the strategic planning process must next turn to assembling those sets of actions, the tactics, that will implement the goals. In the world of finance, this will demand a review of the possible financing structures and sources of funds that may be available. Such an identification process is where much of the creativity in financial management and planning is now located. The problem here is one of designing cash-raising solutions to meet programmatic goals in the volatile context of changing financial, political and economic environments with a shifting set of internal constraints. The identification of alternatives is the first step of financial analysis. But it is well to remember that it is also a step that may need to be repeated frequently over the life of a strategic plan that has multiple goals covering a long time period. What may make eminently good sense at one stage may prove impractical or uneconomical down the road, as the environment, internal conditions or the goals themselves are altered. By the same token, an approach that may appear at first glance to be overly complicated or downright uneconomical may over time evolve into the best possible solution under different circumstances.

Analyzing financing alternatives: short-term versus long-term

Reduced to its most basic elements, the financing alternatives can be reviewed as those decisions that involve: (1) the raising of funds from various sources and (2) their allocation among alternative uses. A framework of analysis is required in coupling these two major areas of choice to accomplish the strategic plan that has been developed. The concepts introduced above regarding the cost of capital, the returns on its use, the risk and reward trade-offs and the need for financial flexibility all come into play when analyzing alternatives. Keep in mind that neither the source nor the allocation of funds can be considered in isolation.

As most government finance officers are concerned with the left side of the equation—the raising of funds—this discussion now turns to an area of particular concern and a practical example: *the decision of short-term versus long-term financing.* The concepts discussed earlier are well illustrated by the decision that governments frequently must make regarding the structuring of their liabilities, and the decision between borrowing on a short- or long-term basis. In today's expensive and volatile capital markets, the usual maxims about aligning obligations with the useful life of a project to be financed, or the inflows of revenues to repay them, may or may not make good economic sense at a given time or for a particular borrower and in a particular market. For example, changing tax laws may influence borrowers who feel threatened by such changes to behave differently than they would if their tax treatment were more secure. Moreover, whatever their decisions are, they may well affect the condition of the market for other borrowers. On several occasions in the past, borrowers that could avoid long-term financings were well advised to do so to avoid the crush of borrowers reacting to special situations such as the sunsetting of particular tax treatments. Certainly, the choices need to be examined in a rational framework and the reasoning retested on a recurring basis in light of current market conditions.

Looking specifically at the short-term borrowing decision, historically it has been true that the tax-exempt yield curve is upward sloping and that short-term borrowing carries a lower rate of interest than long-term bonds. Were governments certain that future short-term rates would always be lower than the prevailing long-term rates, then it might appear that continuously borrowing in the short-term market would be the only alternative. Actually, the assumption regarding future rates need not be all that strong. Were a government convinced that over the next few years short-term rates would be lower than current long-term rates, it might well save enough in near-term interest costs to offset higher long-term rates and debt service costs in the future. This is because of the higher present value of the savings it would be enjoying today.

But there are practical limits to the use of short-term financing, and most of them revolve around the magnitude of the financing and the purposes for which borrowing is done. For most government capital financings, the level of risk entailed in prolonged and exclusive use of short-term financing has proved to be unacceptable—large floating debt typically has exposed a government to constant remarketing and continual worries about future market access and interest costs. Thus, short-term debt traditionally has been tied to cash flow concerns, where sufficient revenues, or a virtually certain funding of the debt by future bond sales or grant receipts, assure that the debt can be repaid when due. Since most financial crises in government have been accompanied by abuses of short-term borrowing, the rating agencies have been particularly wary of growing accumulations of short-term debt and most interested in the plan for its prompt and definite repayment.

Short-term borrowing, then, can be a tool to accomplish near-term flexibility, so long as the means of its repayment are clearly in sight and close at hand. But, its accumulation over time can greatly reduce future flexibility, because of the constant recourse that must be made to the financial markets. There is a risk, typically not found in long-term financing, that the overall cost of credit will be greater due to errors in timing or credit concerns, and the uncertainty that accompanies not knowing what future debt service will be. The importance of these concerns essentially is rooted in the nature of the investment that the borrowing finances.

If the expenditure is for a major facility that will not produce any immediate revenues for the government, then the existence of large unfunded debt may represent a potentially dangerous situation. On the other hand, where the debt is matched by a highly liquid asset or large flow of dependable revenue or receipts of assured availability, then the use of short-term borrowing appears much less risky and the interest cost savings more attractive. This is not to suggest that use of short-term obligations—especially hybrids such as variable-rate demand bonds—is an inappropriate means to finance capital projects.

Indeed, the accessing of short-term tax-exempt markets to finance capital is increasing, and is by no means imprudent given proper safeguards. The credit and market risks associated with short-term borrowing can be alleviated by use of credit backstops and bank liquidity facilities and the market risk of flexible-rate debt can be partially or totally offset through use of interest rate hedges and interest rate ceiling insurance.

The ideal, of course, is the "arbitrage situation" where short-term liabilities are directly offset by equally short-term assets that produce revenues in excess of the interest cost they entail. However, the opportunities for such ideal applications of short-term borrowing are under constant assault by the U.S. Treasury and congressional tax-writing committees. An interesting variation of this risk is the risk of falling interest rates leading, in the extreme condition, to negative arbitrage against fixed-rate debt. Be that as it may, it does illustrate that when short-term borrowing is used to acquire financial assets, rates of return on that investment also need to be considered.

Applying strategic planning

Having identified the concepts of strategic financial planning, the question arises: What about the planning process itself as it would apply to short-term financing techniques? Examination of the environment is particularly important, since the choice will be governed in part by interest rate expectations. Not only are the levels of rates themselves of consequence, but also of consequence is the relationship between long and short rates, taxable and tax-exempt rates, and the returns on temporarily invested proceeds. These and other environmental features are beyond the government's control.

Assessing the current situation the government faces is important in deciding if it is financially and institutionally capable of taking on the risks inherent in short-term financing and, if so, in determining the acceptable limits of such risks when compared with the likely interest cost savings (or arbitrage earnings). For example, given the market's perception of the credit quality of the issuer, will liquidity backstops and credit enhancements be needed, and if so, to what extent? Will the cost of these financial facilities and enhancements, and possible constraints they may place on the government's operations, be acceptable? Or, given the use of the funds being raised, would the issuer be accepting too much risk of future illiquidities? Is there a responsible member of the staff with sufficient skill to oversee and manage short-term financings on a recurring basis (this is a concern in commercial paper programs)?

Setting goals and constraints will, in turn, provide a framework for identifying and choosing alternative courses of action. Ideally, general parameters should be constructed that set out the acceptable limits for use of short-term borrowing and allowable risks and priorities. A general decision to borrow on a short-term basis leads to a consideration of a multitude of alternative borrowing vehicles, which encompass a range of demand and variable-rate securities that have gained considerable popularity and promise the greatest interest savings. But, the interest savings entail the cost of absorbing more risk and applying more sophistication (and resources) to the short-term borrowing process.

It is absolutely critical to realize that the short-term vs. long-term decision is not simply a matter of doing or not doing a demand note or a commercial paper program. All of the particular risks associated with both raising and using funds can be addressed within the context of the individual borrower, and can be mitigated in a multitude of ways. But, the choice of short-term borrowing places a continuing responsibility on the issuer to be vigilant as to market trends and the possible option of funding out when the optimal time comes. The time and talent those future decisions will take need to be figured into the process.

Conclusion

The celebrated fiscal adversities of the past few years—taxpayer revolts, deep recessions, federal aid cutbacks and unsettled bond markets—have sorely tested the wit and energy of government financial managers. Overall, the managers have met the tests, and state and local governments have demonstrated flexibility and resiliency in the face of unrelenting and often unexpected change.

There seems to be little prospect that finance officers will find their professional world returning to the more routine and predictable. Thinking differently and creatively about the job and the many crosswalks which link how funds are raised, stored and used by governments will be imperative in retaining the fiscal resiliency of state and local finance.

The 1986 Tax Reform Act and the Financial Future of Cities

Douglas D. Peterson and Donald R. Winkler

The lengthy national debate on tax reform ended on September 26, 1986, when the U.S. Congress passed the Tax Reform Act of 1986 and forwarded the bill to President Reagan for signature. Like all legislation, the tax bill was a political compromise, but the major goals of tax reform—lower marginal tax rates on personal income and a broader tax base—were achieved. The question now is what the effects of the tax reform will be on individuals, businesses, and state and local governments. This article examines some of the potential long-run effects of tax reform on municipal finance.

The Tax Reform Act of 1986

The 1986 tax reform is landmark legislation, creating the most significant changes in the federal income tax since World War II.[1] The legislation is characterized by three major elements: (1) tax payments by individuals are reduced by about $120 billion over five years, while tax payments by businesses are raised by approximately the same amount, resulting in a "revenue neutral" reform; (2) marginal and average tax rates are reduced for most individuals, while tax rates are increased for businesses; and (3) the tax bases for both individuals and businesses are broadened by, among other things, reducing tax shelter opportunities for individuals and reducing cost recovery on capital investments by business.

Municipal finances are most directly affected by the measures taken to expand the individual and business tax bases. Most of the specific measures directly affecting cities involve issuance of tax-exempt debt.[2] These measures include (1) more narrowly defining what constitutes a "public purpose" for issuing tax-exempt debt, (2) lowering statewide volume caps on issuance of "private purpose" tax-exempt debt, (3) subjecting some holders of "private purpose" bonds to an individual "minimum" tax on interest income, (4) defining most tax-increment redevelopment bonds as industrial development bonds (IDBs) subject to the statewide cap, (5) eliminating the interest deduction formerly taken by banks carrying government debt (excepting debt of small cities), and (6) further limiting opportunities to earn income through arbitrage.

Impact of tax reform on local government

The Tax Reform Act of 1986 affects both sides of the municipal ledger—revenues on one hand and the costs of providing services on the other. While many of these effects can be identified, the magnitude of their importance is almost impossible to predict. Furthermore, even ten years after enactment it may not be possible to assess the precise effects of the act due to the confounding influence of a large number of other environmental changes that will assuredly affect local government financial conditions.[3] Changes in the rate of economic growth, in federal transfers to states and cities, and in state mandates to cities may all occur in the near future, affecting municipal financial conditions in ways that cannot be easily distinguished from the effects of the tax act.

This examination of the effects of the Tax Reform Act is, in the parlance of public finance economists, a partial equilibrium analysis. In other words, only those tax changes that have a relatively strong and obvious impact on municipal finance are considered. An example is the change in federal regulations regarding issuance of tax-exempt bonds.

While this analysis is necessarily limited to specific tax changes and their effects, the reader should be aware of the possibility that the more general effects of the tax change may have a great impact on local governments. One possible example is the elimination of consumer interest deductions (except for mortgages and some home equity loans), which will lead to higher after-tax (to the borrower) loan rates, which may result in reduced loan demand and, consequently, lower interest rates, which may be reflected in lower interest rates on the bonds issued by cities. Each tax change contained in the act has some impact, however small, on municipal finance. Taken together, these general effects of the tax change may be more important than the more specific effects examined here.

The analysis that follows considers the impact of the Tax Reform Act on revenues (through its effects on the tax base, tax rates, and choice of taxes), costs of providing services, and intergovernmental fiscal relations. Only the principal source of municipal own-source tax revenues—the property tax—is considered here. Similarly, only the capital costs component of service provision is considered. Finally, two aspects of intergovernmental fiscal relations are discussed—intergovernmental transfers and state regulation of tax-exempt financial markets.

The property tax base   The Tax Reform Act could change the local tax base by affecting both the level and growth of property values. The impact of the act on home values is indeterminate. While the decrease in personal income tax rates increases the after-tax price of home ownership (and thus may reduce demand for and property values of owner-occupied homes), this effect may be offset by the elimination of other shelters. In addition, the increase in disposable family income should also result in increased demand for housing.

The impact of the act on the values of rental units is likely to be negative. The reduced cost recovery provisions (less generous depreciation, elimination of the investment tax credit) of the Tax Reform Act will reduce the profits and in fact produce losses for many owners of rental units, unless there is a large shift in demand from home ownership to rental units. The net result is likely to be a reduction in property values of rental units and/or a reduction in property values of owner-occupied homes. The adjustment to lower property values may take some time, but in the long run cities are likely to observe lower growth in the value of already developed residential property than would have occurred without the act.

The effects of the act on the values of commercial and industrial real estate also are likely to be negative. Again, the reduced cost recovery provisions of the act will yield actual (not just paper) losses, which will be reflected in reduced property values for many owners. Furthermore, this reduction in economic rent should be capitalized in lower prices for undeveloped land as well.

In addition to lower property values, the act is likely to reduce the rate of real estate development in many cities. To the extent that the reduction in economic rent is immediately and fully capitalized in lower land values, the rate of development will not be adversely affected. But, as is more likely, if the process by which real prices of land fall takes time, developers will wait until the demand for existing commercial and industrial space raises rental prices sufficiently to produce economic gain for new developments.

The Tax Reform Act is likely to reduce both the existing property tax base and the rate of growth in the property tax base. Yet it is possible that the general equilibrium effects of the act, in particular the incentives to increase personal savings, may result in lower interest rates, which partially or fully offset the negative effects of reduced cost recovery on property values and development.

The tax rate   The Tax Reform Act also can influence the decisions made by voters or their elected representatives about tax rates. Once again, countervailing forces are at work. The reduced federal income tax burden on individuals will leave voters with more disposable income, part of which they may choose to spend (through higher tax rates) on public services. On the other hand, the reduction in marginal tax rates on the federal income tax serves to increase the after-tax price of public services for most voters.

The ambiguity facing individuals does not apply to businesses, most of which will experience both a reduction in after-federal tax profits and an increase in the after-tax price of local public services. The reduction in after-tax profits results from higher taxes paid on a broadened tax base. The increase in the after-tax price of local public services results from the reduction in maximum nominal corporate tax rates (from 46 percent to 34 percent).

Choice of taxes   In addition to influencing tax rate levels, the Tax Reform Act influences tax choice, disallowing deductibility of sales tax payments for taxpayers who itemize. Cities in 27 states plus the District of Columbia currently use the sales tax. In 1983, cities received $12.7 billion in sales tax revenue, with cities in California and New York accounting for almost half the total.

Under the act, for a given local tax payment, the after-federal tax burden to itemizers will be higher under use of a sales tax than under use of a property tax. As a result, over time there should be some shift away from use of the local sales tax in favor of other revenue sources. States such as California, which have strictly limited local property tax revenues, may now find strong arguments for relaxing those limitations.

Costs of providing services   The most important changes of the Tax Reform Act on the cost of providing local government services are those affecting the issuance of and market for tax-exempt debt.[4] These changes limit the purposes for which tax-exempt debt can be issued and thereby should reduce the supply of tax-exempt debt to the market. The cost of those activities that can still be financed via tax-exempt debt will be reduced relative to those that must now be financed via taxable debt. One may thus find changes in the mix of activities and services provided by cities. Compared with the past, cities may provide fewer of those services no longer eligible for tax-exempt bond status, including multifamily housing, convention facilities, and tax-increment-financed redevelopment projects.

While the supply of tax-exempt debt to the market should decline, the demand for tax-exempt debt may also fall due to the decrease in marginal tax rates on the federal income tax. The net effect on the spread in yields between tax-exempt and taxable debt is indeterminate.[5]

Intergovernmental fiscal relations   The most obvious impact of the Tax Reform Act on intergovernmental fiscal relations is the reduced volume cap on private purpose bonds.[6] For the 29 states where 1985 issues exceed the new cap, state government serves the role of arbiter in determining which local governments can issue bonds for which purposes. Hence, the impact of the act is to centralize local government bond funding decisions at the state level.

Ironically, for a few states that have issued a large volume of tax-exempt private purpose bonds in the past, the consequences of the act may be decentralizing. In 1985, for example, Colorado issued almost six times and California issued almost four times as many private purpose bonds as are permitted under the new volume cap. Local governments in these states may need to resort to the taxable bond market to continue to meet their funding needs and, hence, need not be subject to the whims of the state bond commission.

The other impact of the act on intergovernmental fiscal relations may be only transitory. In the absence of new state legislation, the act, through its base-broadening provisions, generates revenue gains for 35 state governments and revenue losses for only three.[7] Revenue gains may in part be transferred to local governments. A more likely outcome, however, is pressure on those state and local governments employing the income tax to revise and simplify their tax codes to be similar to the new federal legislation.

Conclusions

There are too many unknowns to predict with confidence the effects of the 1986 Tax Reform Act on municipal finances. The act will affect the property tax base and may also affect decisions about property tax rates. It will increase the cost of providing some municipal services and should lead to different mixes in the services supplied. And the act may provide an important impetus for tax revision at both the state and local levels. Finally, whatever the real effects on municipal finance, one can be confident that many unrelated changes in municipal fiscal conditions will in fact be attributed to the Tax Reform Act.

1. U.S. Congress, Joint Committee on Taxation, *Summary of Conference Agreement on H.R. 3838 (Tax Reform Act of 1986)* (Washington, D.C.: U.S. Government Printing Office, 1986).
2. *The Bond Buyer,* 19 August 1986.
3. Douglas D. Peterson, *City Fiscal Conditions in 1986* (Washington, D.C.: National League of Cities, 1986).
4. "Tax Agreement Will Curtail Bonds," *Nation's Cities Weekly,* 25 August 1986.
5. Jeffrey I. Chapman and Donald R. Winkler, "Tax-Exempt Debt: An Intergovernmental Perspective," *American Review of Public Administration,* 1986.
6. "Tax Reform's Bond Caps Too Low for 29 States," *City and State,* October 1986.
7. "States Scramble to Gauge Effect of Tax Changes," *New York Times,* 5 October 1986.

PART 2

Stimulating Future Economic Growth

Trends for Economic Development

Richard Erickson

Greatness in anything, from sand castles to skyscrapers, doesn't just happen: it must be achieved. And ultimately, great cities—whether large or small—reflect the vision and aspirations of the local leaders who guide and govern them. For municipal leaders charged with guiding the urban development of their turf, a new set of trends—and a new set of rules for using them—is forming on the economic horizon.

What does a city require to ensure it will grow enough to remain healthy? There are many variables, and they can be equally important—desire for growth, the room to grow, a commitment to enhancing the quality of life, vital economic resources, and enough continued effort to ensure the requisite luck.

Take, for example, the list of needs that General Motors Chairman Roger Smith presented to cities across America vying for his $5 billion commitment to the Saturn automobile. When all the other plans were presented, the chief consideration on Smith's mind was for a place to put his state-of-the-art, computerized plant, a plant that would, on-site, employ 6,000 workers. That kind of development can turn a community around.

Phones in Detroit began ringing from the moment GM made the announcement. City officials all over the country pulled incentives out of their briefcases and started booking airline tickets. Kansas City offered 300 acres of prime land free of charge. The governor of Illinois rushed to GM headquarters to make a pitch, leaving just as Michigan's governor arrived.

But a number of the hundreds of communities desperately

Reprinted with permission from *American City & County*, October 1985.

seeking Saturn—which ultimately went to tiny Spring Hill, Tennessee, a hamlet of 1,100 souls that didn't even make a presentation—had not felt a need to pull a marketing effort together overnight. For them, GM was just another client—the one that got away.

These cities have learned a valuable lesson: These days, economic development is a vital business in the public sector. And officials who sit back and wait for new jobs and developments to wander into town are going to be doing a lot of sitting. The key is to go out and find the seeds for growth.

High-technology companies, even with the slump in the industry, are still prime targets. They are "clean," teach valuable skills to local residents and, by their very presence, tend to attract more of their kind to the community.

Leaders in Washington state, not necessarily known as the heart of high tech, have begun a quiet but effective campaign for those jobs. Consider the success garnered by the city of Camas, Washington, where plans for a $200 million RCA/Sharp Microelectronics semiconductor plant are well underway.

"The reason we were so successful in bringing RCA/Sharp Microelectronics to Camas stems from a concerted team effort on the part of the city, state officials and the Columbia River Economic Development Council (CREDC)," notes Mike Parker, assistant city engineer.

"We had a series of meetings; they would come up with questions; we would meet and come up with proposals and solutions. At one point, RCA/Sharp was concerned about the cost of the needed sewer structures. Against an anticipated $5.5 million system estimated by another party, we proposed a $1.3 million sewer to service the plant's high-volume water consumption. They were still hesitant, however, until I offered a design with dual reliability, based on a second route, for $1.7 million," says Parker.

The ample local water supply and good climate, combined with city and country teamwork, out-maneuvered eight other suitors seeking the semiconductor plant. Director of Public Works Mel Avery, Finance Director Dale Scarbrough, Mayor Nan Henricksen and CREDC President Joe Tanner each showed that by working together they could provide the needed answers for success.

One of the locations RCA/Sharp considered before deciding on Camas was Colorado Springs, Colorado, a community quickly gaining its spurs in high-tech economic development.

Attracted by the promise of land, nearby educational facilities and a compatible business environment, the roster of firms located in Colorado Springs sounds as if it were plucked from the pages of *In Search of Excellence:* Ampex, AVX, Data General, Digital Equipment, Ford Aerospace, Gates Data, Hewlett-Packard, Honeywell, Hotsy, Inmos, Litton, Mostek, NCR, IBM's ROLM, Systems Development, Texas Instruments, TRW and United Technologies.

But the situation was not always so rosy for the mountain community. In the early 1970s, Colorado Springs was deteriorating, living mainly on tourist and defense dollars from Fort Carson, Peterson Air Force Base and the Air Force Academy. The local private sector, primarily developers, decided to change the course of the city and formed a flying business circus. This group began a systematic campaign of traveling slide shows shown to everyone from financiers in New York to technocrats in Texas to growing companies along the clogged freeways of Silicon Valley. The results of this effort, coupled with local government cooperation—and specifically the economic development arm of the Chamber of Commerce—have proved enormously successful.

"Unlike many areas, we are charting our own course," says James Devine, director of economic development for Colorado Springs' Chamber of Commerce. With some grounds for the overstatement, Devine adds: "Colorado Springs is writing the book on economic development."

Ripping the red tape

A page, perhaps, from that same book is being written by Lowell, Massachusetts. In the 1800s, Lowell was known as Spindle City, with a number of prosperous textile mills. By 1950, the textile manufacturers had begun to move south in search of cheaper labor costs. They left behind a grim place, filled with stagnant canals, boarded-up mills and weeds cascading over cracked courtyards.

In 1975, Lowell's far-sighted mayor began reversing the stagnation, designating some of the city's crumbling mills as Heritage State Park. Three years later, a senator who grew up in Lowell cajoled Congress into proclaiming the area a national historic park and bringing in $40 million in federal funds to restore the old mills.

As rejuvenation began, a group of local political leaders and executives decided to keep the economic ball rolling by persuading all 10 banks in the area to capitalize a development corporation to provide the riskier end of redevelopment financing. The city then agreed to slash the red tape that can sometimes retard the spark of building renovation.

In all of these examples, the interplay of needs on the part of the business sector and the ability of local leaders to satisfy those needs forms a fabric of possibilities upon which trends in economic development begin to work. Whether trying to revitalize urban development, or simply trying to bring new blood into the metropolitan community, certain known attributes are desirable, including: available labor, nearby educational facilities, climate, energy costs, effective transportation, quality of life and a moderate cost of living. While any of these may end up being more important to a particular project or firm, local governments that are successful in economic development work to provide all of them. Thus, throughout the nation, individual communities are having to tailor their thrusts in economic development.

Signs of success

In Texas, there is a corridor of communities that seem to bring all the ingredients necessary for successful development together. Dallas, Houston, Austin and San Antonio all have established programs that have garnered healthy economic returns and provide actions worthy of emulating by other localities. While local governments there may be faced with a new set of problems in the wake of so much success, the positive effects on their respective communities far outweigh any new challenges.

Dallas has focused its primary effort around its reputation as a major corporate headquarters community. Here, the largest chamber of commerce in the nation, with a membership of 8,000, maintains a firm grip on the area's economic development.

According to Kathy Dixon, manager of the Chamber's Business Development Division, so much development is proposed each year that her department's primary role is to act as a clearinghouse for business prospects. When a company calls for information, Dixon explains, the request is passed through to one of the appropriate member corporations who assist in the initial stages.

Riding such a wave of success, few people have been surprised that Dallas has no current marketing effort to bring new business to town. Yet, Dixon believes this will soon change. She points out that the Chamber has ordered an economic indicators study, aimed at pinpointing exactly what today's executives want from the community. "Hopefully," notes Dixon, "what will come of it will help the Chamber be more active instead of reactive. We can't sit here and rely on our name; we have to get out there, too."

A recent trend Dixon sees recurring in the Dallas area is that more corporate moves require their own criteria evaluation. This is good and bad for local government officials because, while it eliminates "tire kickers"—the corporate site selectors who are just in the preliminary stages of development considerations—corporate perceptions of Dallas are already in place. Naturally, those perceptions may also not be entirely positive or correct.

On the other side of the state, Houston civic leaders watching the price of oil continue to slip are becoming more aggressive in marketing the city.

Dick Bryant of the Houston Economic Development Council relates that it has been important to discover the non-oil assets that Houston has to offer. The Port of Houston, for example, is now the most active deep-water port in the country in foreign tonnage, and because of that, Houston is the largest center of international trade and finance in the Sunbelt. While important to the oil industry, this fact is also a development tool that can be leveraged in many other business sectors. Such self-examination could be utilized to good advantage anywhere in the nation.

The space program offered another economic vista to the city. Spin-offs from the nearby Johnson Space Center are becoming more powerful as the commercialization of outer space leaves the pages of science fiction and enters the business and government sections of the local press. "We are going out to the rest of the world and saying it is time for your business to look at space, because it is possible to manufacture there and experiment there and improve products on Earth by lessons learned in space," notes Bryant. And spin-offs from oil and space research have created a high-tech push that is new to Houston.

Too much success?

Dealing with economic growth has presented a different set of challenges to local officials and Chamber of Commerce members in Austin, Texas. With its deep base of academia and growing reputation as a high-tech center, Austin is not as aggressive as Houston. In fact, according to Angelos Angelou, vice president of the Economic and Business Development Division of the Austin Chamber of Commerce, the city's effort is singularly reactive: "We do not actively seek new business. One of the successes of the Austin development division is that its best marketing system is the absence of one." Clearly, there is another lesson to be learned from Austin.

With the benefits of new and better-paying jobs comes the need for planning. Austin, controlled in the late 1970s by a community element that wanted no more growth, did not do much planning, expecting that the lack of infrastructure would slow its boom-town reputation. But companies came anyway.

As a result, Austin now faces a shortage of low-cost housing, a lack of utilities for some of the new areas, tremendously overcrowded highways and regular problems thanks to overloaded sewage treatment plants. Late in 1984, a $1 billion bond issue was finally passed by the citizenry, but the money will only be enough to catch up with the city's growth. And more is coming—despite the community's seemingly casual attitude toward economic development.

Thus, Austin tends to sell itself naturally, in contrast to Dallas, which is concerned about marketing efforts, and Houston, which is actively courting new businesses. Austin has sat back and let the companies come to it.

Austin leaders believe that excellent educational facilities and a laid-back lifestyle act as magnets, bringing business developments that suit the setting, such as IBM, Motorola, Texas Instruments and Microelectronic and Computer Technology Corporation (MCC). Obviously, managing and planning community attributes is an integral key to balanced, long-term growth. With 31 percent of adults living in the city having more than 16 years of education—the highest rate of any city in the nation—the ability to cope with growth challenges is apparent. But long-term planning is going to be crucial if Austin's quality of life is to be maintained.

An ongoing challenge

In San Antonio, Texas, 75 miles south of Austin, recognizing the limitations of established economic advantages is an ongoing challenge. The city has five military bases and a healthy tourist trade forming the traditional base of its economy, yet city leaders have noted since the end of the Vietnam War that San Antonio needed to diversify.

This has largely been accomplished by the San Antonio Economic Development Foundation (SAEDF), in cooperation with local government, which has changed the economic face of the city during the last decade. At the same time, the focus of the foundation's efforts has changed as the texture of San Antonio has changed. The city's first tool company and national garment manufacturer were seen as catalysts for sparking new manufacturing skills in the community. And the electronics industries that have followed are using some of those same type skills. And yet, Stephanie Coleman, SAEDF president, says that the city must guard against tying too many of its ships to a single anchor.

"When we look at our track record," notes Coleman, "I suppose that the larger announcements have been in the area of electronics. But we see the electronics industry in a tremendous slump right now. We see the impact that slump has had on Austin, on Colorado Springs, on Phoenix, on all areas heavily dependent on electronics companies for new investments for existing jobs. It is obvious that the electronics industry is going to come back and this is just one of the down cycles, but we are trying to get away from being so dependent on one or two aspects of the economy as we once were."

Another challenge was addressed when MCC selected Austin in place of San Antonio. San Antonio had been among the five finalists but lost out because, while its cost of living and quality of life were excellent, its higher educational facilities were not as strong as Austin's. The loss of MCC threw San Antonio's leaders, notably Mayor Henry Cisneros, onto a new track. If the city was not strong in high-tech educational facilties, what was it strong in?

Finding that answer uncovered a deep resource in medical and biological research facilities, a strong military medical tradition and top-notch independent research firms in other fields. Out of this realization came San Antonio's plan to pursue a future in biotechnology—the linkage of life sciences to industry.

At the same time, the prospect is somewhat frightening: using San Antonio's educational and research resources to recruit new companies, which will, in turn, create products as yet unthought of, products that hopefully will be profitable and stimulate new jobs. The situation can be compared to traveling down a road parallel to a railroad track, knowing that somewhere down the line the road and tracks will cross and, sometime soon, there is a train coming.

"This is going to be for the long haul," says Coleman. "It is part of the growth of the future. The promise of the industry is that it is going to be so vibrant, so fast-growing that, when the next phase with production is reached, it is going to grow like wildfire and have the resources of embryonic companies to be started here. Certainly it takes a while, but if it is going to be part of our growth, part of the growth of this city, we are in it for the long haul, and we are starting now."

Key strategies

This ambitious, aggressive stance is one of the key ingredients to San Antonio's growth and its economic development effort. It is, in fact, one of the city's primary resources—one that cities throughout the country can adopt for their own.

Cities have become more and more competitive in trying to gain their lion's share of new business. The competition is stiff, so the tactics will be intensified. And if the "marketing" of a city is still regarded by some as progressive, the time is not far away when cities may be marketed like breakfast cereal—where success may depend on the surprise inside the box.

But beyond this, there are today evolving trends that are bringing success to urban development programs across America. Whether it is the teamwork of Camas, the hard sell of Colorado Springs, the fund procurement of Lowell, the re-examination of economic thrusts in Houston or the bold planning of San Antonio, the efforts are beginning to reap success.

Why Local Governments Need an Entrepreneurial Policy

William Schweke

Local governments across the nation must tailor new and more innovative entrepreneurial policies. Without them, they will not create an adequate supply of jobs. Attracting outside firms or holding onto their existing business base is not enough for the 1980s.

The American economy is undergoing one of the most fundamental transformations in its history. The landscape is being altered by three monumental shifts: from an industrial to an informational economy, from a cheap and abundant supply of natural resources to an expensive and constricting supply, and from an insular national economy to an interdependent one.

To address the turmoil and loss of jobs caused by these forces, economic adjustment measures and the retention of still viable firms are not enough. New jobs must be generated, and new directions in economic development policy must be sought.

Attracting outside firms

State and local governments have a long history of pursuing a plan to attract outside firms—a strategy sometimes referred to as smokestack chasing. The principal vehicles used have been tax incentives and other financing mechanisms, labor force training, and infrastructure investments. Recently, however, the value of these mechanisms has been questioned. Several empirical studies have found little evidence that tax incentives are decisive in determining where corporations locate facilities.

Despite these problems, business attraction strategies remain an important element of a community's economic development policy. Attracting new firms in a different industrial sector can help to

Reprinted with permission from the December 1985 issue of *Public Management* magazine, published by the International City Management Association.

diversify an area's economic base. And the improvements in an area's business climate required in such a strategy can enhance its comparative advantages, ideally generating more wealth and added economic efficiency overall.

The potential of new enterprise development

Most local governments will not create an adequate supply of jobs by merely attempting to attract outside firms or retain the existing business base: They must aggressively attempt to foster new enterprise development. Indeed, an economy adjusts to change by spawning new businesses.

Sources of job generation Researchers from both the Massachusetts Institute of Technology (MIT) and the Brookings Institution have discovered that slightly more than 50 percent of all new jobs between 1969 and 1980 were created by independent small entrepreneurs. This figure far exceeds such employers' 37-percent share of total jobs. New and young establishments are also responsible for a majority of jobs created, a fact that applies to all facilities, whether independent, subsidiaries, or branch plants.

Brookings also discovered that small independent concerns generated 264 percent of net employment change in the 1980–82 period.

These findings indicate that small independent businesses contribute more than half their share of baseline employment. They also demonstrate that the small business share of employment growth varies by the time period analyzed.

The surprisingly large role of young firms in job creation is reflected in a detailed case study of the electronics industry. The American Electronics Association surveyed its member corporations to measure the growth rate of firms in four different age categories: mature (more than 20 years old), teenage (between 10 and 20 years old), and developing (5 to 10 years old), and start-ups (less than 5 years old). For 1976, the survey found that the average employment growth rate for the teenage companies was from 20 to 40 times the rate for mature companies. Developing companies had an employment growth rate in 1976 that was nearly 55 times the growth rate for mature companies. The growth rate for start-ups in 1976 was 115 times that of mature companies.

A U.S. General Accounting Office (GAO) study of the venture capital industry points out that $209 million in venture capital investments in the 1970s created 130,000 jobs, more than $100 million in corporate tax revenues, $350 million in employee tax revenues, and $900 million in export sales.

Profitability On the whole, small businesses appear to be as profitable as, if not more profitable than, large corporations. Economist

Michael Kieschnick discovered in a study of manufacturing firms that businesses with less than $5 million in assets were just as profitable as firms with assets over $1 billion. The study, using data from the Federal Trade Commission (FTC), covered the years from 1958 to 1976. In the last five years, small firms substantially outperformed large ones. For example, between 1972 and 1976, U.S. manufacturing corporations with assets under $1 million produced an average after-tax return on equity of 15.95 percent, while firms with assets over $1 billion returned only 12.91 percent. (The FTC figures include failures.) A later study by Kieschnick covering the 1977–80 period found that firms with less than $5 million in assets have consistently been more profitable than any other size class of manufacturing firms.

Other research confirms these results. In a study of 38 venture capital funds, the State of California Economic Policy Department found that the average return from 1960 to 1980 was 25.7 percent per year.

Sources of new products and industrial innovation   Small business plays a critical role in new technological innovation. The U.S. Department of Commerce concluded in a 1967 study, *Technological Innovation: Its Environment and Management*, that more than 50 percent of all scientific and technological developments since the beginning of the century could be directly attributed to the efforts of small businesses and independent inventors. Small firms and independent inventors not only are the main source of innovation, however; they also seem to innovate more efficiently and at a lower cost than larger firms. The National Science Foundation has reported that, from 1953 to 1973, small enterprises produced 4 times as many innovations per research and development dollar as medium-sized firms, and 24 times as many as large businesses.

A GAO investigation reviewed nine major empirical studies on this issue, concluding that smaller firms contribute mightily to industrial innovation. Their innovative efficiency appears to be higher than that of large firms. Small enterprises also are the most likely contributors to new product development in atomistic industries, while in concentrated industries, they play a more complementary role, performing specialized functions and developing products for bigger business. Finally, some data indicate that small businesses are better at creating new technically feasible ideas than they are at commercializing them. This may partially reflect the capital and other market barriers that small and new and young firms face in the business world, however.

Small firms also tend to innovate in a different manner: They tend to create new products and processes, establishing new markets and hence new jobs; large-firm innovation is directed more at improving efficiencies in production processes and substituting capital for expensive labor, in order to undercut the competition and increase the firm's share of an existing market. Small firms create markets and jobs; large firms often reduce the need for labor in existing markets—ideally, freeing resources for new investment. Other studies suggest that entrepreneurial companies tend to produce more breakthrough creations, while established companies stick to incremental improvements.

Fostering economic resilience   Continuing economic health depends upon the economic vitality represented by a high rate of company formations. "What we really want," business professor Albert Shapero notes, "is to achieve a state denoted by resilience—the ability to respond to changes in the environment effectively; creativity and innovativeness—the ability and willingness to experiment and innovate; initiative taking—the desire and power to begin to carry through useful projects. Preceding and accompanying these dynamic characteristics . . . is diversity. Obviously, diversity offers an area some measures of invulnerability of the effects of many unforeseen events and decisions; unaffected by changes in a single industry or market place or legal constraints on a given product. Less obvious, but perhaps as important, diversity provides a favorable environment for creativity and innovativeness."

Community responsiveness   Small businesses also tend to be more dependent on and responsive to the communities in which they are located. Both the MIT and Brookings studies suggest that smaller firms constitute a particularly important source of growth in stagnating regional and local economies (and declining industries). Thus, for example, at precisely the time the overall steel industry is in rapid decline, several new specialty steel fabricators are experiencing rapid growth.

Studies also have shown that locally controlled businesses increase employment at a faster rate than absentee-controlled firms. Investigations in Wisconsin and Nebraska suggested that, when within-state corporations merge with absentee firms, the growth rate of jobs and income decreases in the areas where the merger occurred. Other research in Maine and Iowa indicates that locally controlled firms increase employment at a faster rate than absentee-owned corporations. This is due to the fact that these larger firms possess greater capital mobility: They operate in a worldwide investment market and therefore have the capability to move anywhere for a higher return. In addition, local firms are much more likely to buy from local suppliers and use area distributors than is a large multiregional operation.

Brookings research discredits the common belief that small

businesses are more volatile and less stable than bigger businesses. This view seems to have no basis; it appears that there is much more turnover of business growth and shrinkage among the largest firms.

Barriers and solutions to enterprise development

Despite the achievement and promise of new enterprise development for renewing economic vitality, starting a new business or expanding a small one is a very difficult undertaking. Seed money and risk-oriented equity investment are often unavailable. Long-term bank debt is scarce. Most traditional sources of government support for business, such as tax incentives, are of little or no help in business formation. Regulatory organizational burdens are disproportionately greater for small and/or young firms.

These systemic barriers also represent opportunities. If once lowered or removed, they provide the opportunity for a widespread increase in new enterprise development, along with associated gains in employment, innovation, and economic development and vitality. Careful identification and assessment of such barriers are critically important. The effectiveness of any public or private policy initiatives to stimulate new enterprise development depends on the existence and significance of the barrier addressed and the appropriateness of the remedy.

While there is not yet a consensus on which of these are most important, we can categorize these barriers according to their association with four of the critical elements of business formation: capital, management, labor, and markets. Some of the major problems and possible solutions follow.

Capital A critical factor in generating new permanent jobs in the private sector is the investment of capital—in the right amount and right form. When capital does not flow to its most productive uses, the economic health of an entire community suffers: New employment is not created, technologies are not developed, and the higher returns of new and profitable enterprise development are not realized.

Existing financial institutions—banks, insurance companies, venture capitalists, investment bankers, and others—appear to work reasonably well for large established corporations. Increasing evidence indicates, however, that appropriate amounts and kinds of capital are not available to all types of business—such as new, young, and small firms.

Present government regulatory practices, fluctuating interest rates, and decontrol of prices, for example, all are combining to inhibit banks from lending long or to small and young firms. A number of existing programs and some new policies, initiated at the local level, can address these problems.

Local initiatives: Local policymakers can encourage and help the private sector to make greater use of Small Business Administration (SBA) programs like the 7A guaranteed loan and 503 Certified Development Company strategy. Trained loan packagers can help local businesses to more effectively access conventional and innovative forms of private and public sector financing. New partnerships between community banks and county pension funds can help commercial banks lend in the long term.

Local governments also can address the seed capital problem. The current system of seed capital financing works well only for the more affluent and for certain high-tech sectors, but this excludes many viable projects. Community seed capital funds can be created (and combined, even more effectively, with small business incubators). Local leaders can attempt to attract outside investors or use the SBA Small Business Investment Company program. The informal capital market of wealthy investors can be improved by computerizing lists of investors and promising entrepreneurs and products and by holding local entrepreneurial networking conferences.

Management   Organizational and management deficiencies comprise another major hurdle to successful business formation. The Small Business Administration asserts that "92 percent of all business failures are a direct result of poor management." In addition, evidence shows that entrepreneurship training actually improves small business performance. During 1971-73, a national demonstration project to stimulate entrepreneurship in nine cities, sponsored by the Small Business Administration, found that businesses whose owners received entrepreneurial training performed better than those whose owners did not. In fact, the evaluation indicated that in these businesses (1) sales increased by 67 percent, (2) net profits increased by 68 percent, (3) personal income increased by 35 percent, and (4) the number of employees increased by 36 percent. Similar findings were reported in another study conducted by the Economic Development Administration. In this five-year experiment, the personal income of the trained group had increased 81 percent, while the personal income among the untrained group had increased by only 19 percent.

Local initiatives: One of the best ways to improve management skills is to establish a small business incubator. An incubator is a business "greenhouse" for nurturing small firms. It is a way to take on a number of small business problems, such as poorly developed entrepreneurial skills; the absence of a good business support infrastructure; the shortage of appropriately sized, reasonably priced, and accessible industrial and commercial premises; and weaknesses in local capital markets, especially for risk capital.

Labor   Inadequate supply or quality of labor can raise costs for business start-ups. The importance of the human capital element in business formation is reflected in the fact that wages represent two-thirds of the value added in the average business.

Local initiatives: Improvements in the local school system and well-run customized training programs can ultimately lower labor costs, enhance productivity, and expand the appropriate supply of skills. Some jurisdictions have even used Comprehensive Employment and Training Act (CETA) and Job Training Partnership Act (JTPA) monies for training individuals to start and run their own businesses. In addition, labor management initiatives have been instrumental in improving the workplace for both parties.

Markets   Failure to study the market thoroughly and inadequate marketing of products are common problems with small, new firms. Larger firms have staff divisions that can monitor the latest technological developments and invest in aggressive and comprehensive marketing strategies. Lack of market knowledge or access can also impede the discovery of good concepts, as well as ways of introducing them.

Local initiatives: Addressing this problem is highly important, since government policy should be concerned not only with accelerating the rate of invention but also with the speed of commercialization and new applications. Some states are computerizing information on new technologies and encouraging new university/business partnerships. Local governments can play some role as an educational go-between for these programs and firms in smaller communities.

Finally, government often has failed to communicate its product and service needs to entrepreneurs in the past. Most new, young, and small firms do not know where to go, whom to address, or how to market their products to the public sector. And for entrepreneurs who are considering going into business, this is an even greater problem. Improved outreach by local and state government agencies for small entrepreneurs and better member education by local chambers of commerce and business affiliations can help substantially.

Conclusion

Local government investments in these areas will leverage additional millions of private sector dollars, creating thousands of enterprises and tens of thousands of new private sector permanent jobs. This is the new frontier of job creation.

Business Incubators: Hatching Jobs and Economic Growth

John Toon

Slightly more than three years ago, the idea for Sales Technologies, Inc., germinated in the minds of Fred Burke, Dennis Crumpler and Chuck Johnson. With their combined backgrounds in consumer product sales and computer technology, these specialists saw potential for a new kind of information system based on the new portable computers just then going into production.

But none of them had ever started a business before. They were unfamiliar with the Atlanta business community where they worked, and needed technical help solving the software problems of the system. So they turned to the Advanced Technology Development Center (ATDC), a business incubator located at the Georgia Institute of Technology in Atlanta.

From the ATDC, the company drew guidance in the nitty-gritty of establishing a business. Through the ensuing program, Burke, Crumpler and Johnson met bankers, attorneys, accountants and Georgia Tech faculty members interested in resolving their software problems. The threesome presented the idea to a group of financiers at an ATDC-sponsored venture capital conference, received business advice from a vice president of a major Atlanta software company, hired Georgia Tech students to work part-time, and rented $5-a-square-foot office space in an old high school renovated by the ATDC.

Today, Sales Technologies employs 28 people in a wood-paneled office tower overlooking one of Atlanta's commercial areas. The company reported revenues of $900,000 for calendar year 1984, and expects $3 million for 1985.

Reprinted with permission from *American City & County*, May 1985.

"The ATDC offered an infrastructure, a helping hand, and a pat on the back that was very important to us," recalls Burke. "The reason a lot of good ideas never get turned into businesses is because people don't know how to go about doing it. It can be overwhelming."

Charles Frazier is president of Digital Devices Corporation, a current ATDC tenant that designs and builds computer peripheral devices. His company used the ATDC's on-site business assistance staff "as a sounding board" for problems and ideas. The company also used the network of business contacts, took advantage of the reasonable rent and hired several Georgia Tech students part-time.

"Being a member of the Development Center meant a lot to us because it gave us a certain amount of prestige and credibility," Frazier says. "We thought about moving, but there are too many benefits here for us to leave."

Small companies like Sales Technologies and Digital Devices—whether high tech, low tech or no tech—account for as many as two-thirds of the new jobs generated in the United States each year. Communities hard hit by the decline of traditional smokestack industries searching for new jobs and economic growth are increasingly looking toward the small business sector, offering support services and financing programs.

Yet nearly half of all small businesses fail within their first five years, making small business boosterism a risky proposition. From the desire to increase the number of small business startups—while improving their chances of success—grew the concept of business incubators.

All shapes and sizes

The University of Minnesota's Humphrey Institute of Public Affairs studied 50 incubator centers in the United States for its July 1984 report on the phenomenon. Later research suggests the number of operating incubators may top 100, with the same number being developed.

Business incubators come in all shapes and sizes. They may be associated with a university, city, county, industry, or set up by a growing number of for-profit corporations licensing their version of the concept. Incubators take root in old schools, factory buildings, post offices and storefronts, renovated with industrial revenue bonds, federal grants or local appropriations. Some provide complete one-stop business assistance service, while others offer bare-bones manufacturing space at rock-bottom prices. Some seek new manufacturing enterprises, while others go after fledgling high-tech companies, service firms or retail ventures. Many early centers were developed to support technology-based companies spinning out of universities.

According to the Humphrey Institute, incubators combat the

two biggest causes of small business problems: under-capitalization and poor business management. They may offer below-market rate rent, on-site business assistance at low cost or no cost, help obtaining financing, share support services such as telephone answering and word processing, provide flexible leases and space arrangements, or "graduation" policies that specify how long companies can stay, along with assisting in the placing and training of employees.

University and industry-based centers can also offer access to superlative, on-site resources such as computer centers, machine shops and libraries at minimal cost.

Minneapolis-based Control Data Corporation operates 16 of what it terms "business and technology centers" across America, making it the largest of six for-profit firms running incubators. And the company has targeted 10 more centers it hopes to open during the remainder of 1985.

"The business and technology center is a kind of focal point for this network of job creation," explains Christelle Langer, manager of communications business development for Control Data. "The business and technology center provides the facilities and service that a small business requires, and provides them at an affordable cost, so those very high initial costs of starting a business are ameliorated."

Control Data believes the availability of seed capital, organized business services and help with business management meet the key needs of its tenants. Shared services like telephone answering, word processing, copying and computer time cut down on overhead costs for individual companies, allowing them to put scarce resources into product or service development, Langer says.

Each center has an on-site manager who can evaluate a company's business plan and offer ongoing assistance. Each is also expected to have a seed capital fund, which can tap into larger corporate resources. Control Data has also established a network among its centers to gain volume-buying discounts and provide a built-in market for tenants' products and services.

Nine of the 16 centers are owned and operated by Control Data. The rest are licensed to communities, which pay the firm for its expertise in getting them started, as well as an annual maintenance fee for continuing support.

Control Data opened its first incubator in Minneapolis five years ago, expecting fledgling high-tech companies as the primary tenants. But it soon found interest more widespread.

"Primarily, our tenants tend to be small service-oriented companies that run to a wide range of businesses," Langer states. "There is a very broad range of entrepreneurs and many viable small businesses. They provide jobs and a good economic base for our communities."

Offering a different approach is the Incubator Industry Building operated by the Buffalo Urban Renewal Agency in Buffalo, New York. Opened in 1978, the project offers 43,000 square feet of industrial space at $2.25 per foot. The structure, built by the city's Public Works Department with a federal Economic Development Administration grant, also includes 3,000 square feet of office and shared service space.

"The basic concept of the project is to encourage new and/or existing growing, light manufacturing businesses to locate in Buffalo, and to foster new manufacturing employment," says Buffalo official David Sengbusch. The low rental rate is aimed at reducing the financial burden of purchasing or constructing manufacturing space.

The initial lease is for one year, with an option to renew for another year. "We anticipate that within that period of time, the tenant will grow sufficiently to warrant the purchase of an existing structure in the city, or in one of our industrial parks," Sengbusch adds. The incubator itself is located in a 40-acre industrial park.

The Akron-Summit Industrial Incubator in Ohio shows the fruits of cooperation between a city, county, university and the private sector.

Located in an old 35,000-square-foot warehouse purchased by the University of Akron, the facility used a combination of city, county, federal and private industry funds for the $352,000 renovation. It now uses a similar consortium of services from the university, the Service Corps of Retired Executives and other sources to provide its business assistance services.

Rent ranges from 50 cents to $2 per square foot, including custodial services and use of a conference room. Shared clerical, bookkeeping, telephone answering, word processing and data processing services are available at low cost to the mixed group of high tech and traditional businesses in the building.

Prospective tenants are reviewed by a panel with representation from each sponsoring group. The panel considers the business plan, financing and potential job creation. Tenants are reviewed every six months, and may stay up to three years if they continue to meet established goals.

Just as existing city, county and university resources can be leveraged to support growing small businesses, so can the facilities of a large manufacturer. The Business Center for New Technology in Rockford, Illinois, grew out of a realization by the Barber-Coleman Company that the services it already provides in-house could be utilized by new businesses, and at a fraction of what they would cost to provide elsewhere.

In the textile machinery company's former corporate headquarters, Barber-Coleman set up office, laboratory and light manufacturing space, allowing fledgling firms to use shared meeting rooms and pay as needed for machine shop, central receiving, computer, model shop, office furnishings, accounting, printing, clerical and telephone answering services.

The whole operation is guided by a Barber-Coleman employee with a business background, who evaluates business plans for tenants and matches them with available services.

St. Paul's experience

When the federal government released emergency job training money to large cities in 1983, many communities used the funds for short-term, make-work public jobs programs. But the city of St. Paul, Minnesota, decided to invest the money in a different way.

"The idea was to put some of that into an incubator that would create jobs that would be long lasting," explains Bob Kessler of the city's Department of Planning and Economic Development. The idea fit in well with the city's "home-grown economy" strategy, a plan that seeks to make the city less dependent on outside corporations for its prosperity.

The city made a deal with a local entrepreneur who had already begun a private incubator, but needed some additional resources—which the city offered. Ultimately, says Kessler, St. Paul leased a portion of the building for its program, opening in January 1984. The facility is now fully leased to small businesses, which pay $1.50 per square foot. The St. Paul small business incubator has been so successful that the city is considering opening another.

The center provides services to its companies, but Kessler believes one of the most valuable contributions is recognition afforded the firms. "It's important for them to feel that somebody cares out there," he says.

His advice to other incubators? "If you are really out to help businesses create jobs, don't expect to make money on it. Don't spend a lot of money to provide services unless they are needed."

Perhaps the oldest and largest incubator program in the United States is the 1.2 million-square-foot University City Science Center in Philadelphia. Begun in 1964 to revitalize a burned-out area of the city, the center draws resources from 28 colleges, universities and medical centers to support 75 companies, government agencies and research groups employing 5,500 persons. In the 20 years since its founding, the center has helped spawn 44 new corporations, serving as a catalyst promoting interaction with the businesses.

Officials estimate that one-third of the center's jobs require no more than a high school education. Minority employment makes up one-fourth of the total jobs, with half of the personnel living in the city.

Services include access to faculty, graduate students and staff from the 28 member institutions; consultation with the center staff;

shared secretarial services; assistance with locating capital; educational seminars; and access to the computer, library and recreational resources of the supporting institutions. The Science Center also maintains a database for locating personnel and consultants in the surrounding area.

The center is part of Pennsylvania's Ben Franklin Partnership, a unique network of agencies organized to encourage innovation and economic development. Pennsylvania, in fact, leads the nation in the number of operating incubator facilities.

Also based in Pennsylvania is Technology Centers International (TCI), which operates several "technology enterprise centers" in the United States. Two distinctive features of incubators developed by this for-profit company include a locally generated venture capital fund of $3.5 million to $5 million, and use of a center "champion" to both manage the incubator and serve as the agent for the venture fund.

This champion evaluates business plans and offers advice to the small companies located in the center. Equally significant, the champion also has access to multiple layers of venture capital, including a "technology master fund" held by the parent company for investments too big for the local seed capital fund.

TCI goes after a mix of start-ups and existing companies, including the attorneys and accounting firms that may provide service to fellow tenants. Its incubator facilities range in size from 40,000 square feet to 60,000 square feet.

Watching for pitfalls

Without question, incubator centers, regardless of their fancy names, can provide attractive contributions to a community—in new jobs, new investment, new development and even renewed community pride. But pitfalls loom for communities that enter the incubator game unaware. Companies like Sales Technologies and Digital Devices are the exceptions, not the rule. Some communities have started business incubators and wished they hadn't.

Candace Campbell, co-author of the Humphrey Institute study and now executive director of the Minnesota Center for Community Economic Development, offers some observations about what incubators should and should not try to do.

"An incubator can only be part of a public entity's overall economic development strategy," Campbell cautions. "It can be used for revitalizing a severely depressed area, or for industrial or job retention, or for new business creation." And she believes that the most successful incubators are those that build a synergism between many agencies and entities concerned with economic development.

"Most business incubators, particularly those that are city or county sponsored, represent a collaboration not only between those public governmental institutions, but also universities, private corporations and lending institutions. It takes a collaborative effort between all the factors in a local economy that are important to small business."

Business incubators, in fact, often result from such a collaborative effort in communities offering small business assistance or financing programs.

"Many of the institutions that have developed incubators are those that have real estate development experience, experience with small business services, or some revolving loan fund for small business," Campbell explains. "Very often, a small business incubator falls out of those things."

Communities that have mastered the art of network-building and service-providing for small business should be able to successfully develop an incubator, Campbell says. She fears, however, that many inexperienced communities may jump into the game and lose.

"Because this is such a sexy thing for cities and counties, everybody wants to have a business incubator," she says. "I think that is fine, but surely there is going to be a lot of fallout. There are going to be a lot of people who develop incubators that are not going to work."

Communities that view a business incubator simply as a way to reuse an old building may also run into trouble. While low rent can be important to fledgling businesses, Campbell argues that business services such as management consulting and help with business planning are critical.

She suggests that cities and counties may not want to become landlords at all, leaving the ownership and management of the physical properties to the private sector. Government, however, can help cut costs by "writing down" the real estate costs.

Screening tenants is also important to ensure a compatible mix and to see that scarce resources are put to best use. But predicting the future of a new company is not a science, and Campbell fears many incubators—especially the for-profits—will pick only those companies most likely to succeed, leaving those with the most need out in the cold.

"It's a real balancing act," she explains. "You really have to guard against skimming the best off the top, the ones that would make it on the outside anyway. But on the other hand, you have to be careful about giving space to people who will never make it."

Tailored to resources

As many as six for-profit corporations provide start-up and management services to communities interested in developing incubators. The firms can offer valuable services, says Campbell, but they must tailor the concept to the community's individual resources.

"It has to be locally sponsored and developed," she suggests. "I don't think that means you cannot use a consultant. But they are going to have to build a rapport with a community so they are a facilitator rather than an owner."

She urges communities to be "good consumers" about the services. Chicago, for instance, sponsored competition to find the three best incubator proposals, to receive $300,000 each. Some 40 proposals came in, Campbell says.

"It's not something you can plop down anywhere and have it work," Campbell concludes. "Each one is different; each one has to be developed differently, and it really depends on the people who have been involved in the development."

Who should operate an incubator? "In most cases, people who have developed successful incubators have been credibly entrepreneurial themselves," says Campbell.

Dr. Fred Tarpley, former director of research for the federal Small Business Administration, now serves as professor and coordinator of economics at Georgia Tech's College of Management. He played an early role in the development of the Advanced Technology Development Center.

"Incubator facilities are most successful when they can leverage existing under-utilized community resources," he says. "It's too expensive to provide lots of one-on-one kind activities from the center, but if you can serve as a network and a focal point in mobilizing the community, that is where it can make the most sense."

Tarpley sees incubators offering an alternative to the traditional economic development tool of industrial recruitment.

"For many years, we spent tremendous amounts of money trying to recruit industry into an area," he notes. "That is basically a zero-sum game, because you have to take it away from somebody to get it. But if a community makes its environment more conducive to business, that doesn't hurt another area. It's a positive-sum game."

Long-term strategy

Tarpley worries that cities and counties starting incubators will look for short-term success measured by a scorecard of companies judged successful.

"You can have a problem of too big an expectation," he warns. "The development process for small business tends to be longer than the political time horizon. Communities are not going to be successful if they are just going to be short-run reactions."

Tarpley views the creation of a business incubator as a statement by the community that small business is important. As such, the center can serve as a focal point, and a magnet, for business activity that reaches far beyond its doors.

"It gives the community resources a place where they can interact, not only in terms of the member firms, but also in terms of the general problems and opportunities that are available."

And Tarpley argues that business incubators should not be expected to make success stories of all the companies they assist.

"The private enterprise system depends on firms entering the marketplace, some failing and some succeeding," he explains. "You want businesses to fail for the right reasons—that their product was inadequate or that they identified the wrong market—not because they lacked access to expertise or didn't get encouragement at the right time. The purpose of an incubator is to improve the environment so that when firms fail, they fail for the right reasons."

Because they have access to a larger pool of resources, Tarpley believes university-based centers will be the most successful.

"University incubators have tremendous knowledge and resources, which they can leverage," he says. "Often, the community incubators are trying to practice entrepreneurship in economically or socially deprived areas. Entrepreneurship is difficult enough without trying to practice it in areas that are distinguished by their lack of resources."

Today the Region, Tomorrow the World

Thomas E. Ward

Any review of techniques for local government involvement in international trade and investment must take into account the relationship between the global economy and the local economy. Because we are a free market economy, consumers and investors in the United States are encouraged to have but one goal—to seek the greatest value for the dollar we spend or the highest rate of return for the dollar we invest. As consumers, we do not generally buy American products just because they are American products. Consequently, local economies in the United States are functions of the global economy to a much greater degree than anywhere else in the world.

Local economic development responds best to the global economy by allowing the same free market forces to guide it that guide the American free market at other levels from the individual to the international. Unfortunately, this is easier said than done, since trade development programs can be difficult to organize and fund without an understanding by the local body politic of the specific relationships between the local economy and the global economy.

It is relatively easy for people to understand that a port needs cranes to put cargo on its ships. It is much more difficult to explain why a locality needs to form an export trading company. It can be especially difficult if the community is located 1,500 miles from an ocean. The programs outlined here are not just for port cities. These programs should be considered by all local governments. Trade development and foreign investment are just as important in Nebraska as they are in Newport News.

Reprinted with permission from the April 1986 issue of *Public Management* magazine, published by the International City Management Association.

It is also important to remember that each local government in a region does not have to "go it alone." In fact, banding together in a regional approach to international economic development is the key to success when dealing with potential trading partners across the globe.

Prerequisites for local international economic development

The initial step in local international economic development is to survey the programs that are in place and available from federal and state governments. These programs vary in size, industrial sector, and effectiveness so much from one area of the country to another that the survey must be conducted locally. The first stop of this review should be the district office of the U.S. Department of Commerce. In putting the local program together, you will be working with limited resources. Avoid duplicating any services that are available from federal and state agencies. After the survey, make sure that everyone in the area is aware of what is available to them from these offices.

Successful local international economic development depends on many of the same techniques as successful domestic economic development. The community must be informed, have an entrepreneurial spirit, and be served by a proactive staff. Programs have to be flexible and responsive. A long-term commitment to "internationalizing" the local economy by the public, business, and academic sectors is required. It may take two or three years to put everything together and produce results.

Successful domestic and international development programs should begin with a very thorough regional economic base study. What is your regional economic base? Is it confined to the local political jurisdiction that you are working in? Probably not. Newport News is the economic center of a region that includes four independent cities and four counties in Virginia. The Newport News International Trade Program serves this entire economic region because of its economic interdependence.

The definition of the regional economic base identifies the economic strengths and weaknesses of any region. Most important, it identifies the best economic opportunities in each locality. These opportunities are what we market both domestically and internationally for new investment. The base study also identifies the existing imports and exports of the regional economy. We seek to replace imports with local activity and expand our exports to other regions, both foreign and domestic.

Once an accurate understanding of the regional economy is achieved, the global perspective must be added. If, from the regional perspective, you identify automobile manufacture as an export opportunity for your region and are unaware that a dozen foreign countries have identified automobile manufacture as a target export industry to this country, you are in serious trouble. If, however, you identify automotive computer components as an export opportunity, you may have a market in the dozen foreign countries trying to export to the United States, as well as a domestic opportunity for your region.

The effective allocation of development resources depends to a great degree on the accuracy of your information. We must be aware of the global market. The free market in the United States is full of indicators that can be used to guide these decisions. The U.S. Department of Commerce, the American press, Wall Street, and the currency markets keep daily records of trade flows. The availability of this information is getting better and better all the time. The speed with which things change also is increasing. Up-to-date, accurate market intelligence is a prerequisite to export development as well as to the attraction of foreign investment.

Once the economic region is defined, an organizational analysis of that region is required: all public offices that are or should be concerned with international economic development; all private sector organizations, from chambers of commerce to Lions Clubs, if appropriate; all academic institutions that are or should be interested and involved. Identify key individuals in these organizations who will garner the support of their organizations to assist in the development and implementation of international programs. Publish and distribute the results of the survey; include trade-, tourism-, and foreign-investment-related offices of state and federal governments.

After going through the processes described here, you should have an objective understanding of the dynamics of your regional economy. It is also important to define the subjective character of your region's people—their heritage, cultural affiliations, and peculiarities. Why is this important? International development, more than almost any other economic activity, is a people business. Experienced traders and other successful international businesspeople all agree that business decisions in the rest of the world rely much more on a concept of trust than anything else. This is not to say that you don't also have to have all your business ducks in a row, but deals are made in the international arena based on trust. Building trust is a matter of interpersonal communication. Foreigners have to like your community, and they have to be able to trust the people involved. The characterization of your region allows you to predict, to a certain extent, what foreign regions are most likely to appreciate your community's character, and vice versa.

We believe that the interregional approach to international co-development is one way the United States can overcome its stagger-

ing problems in international trade. For want of any other termin-
ology, we call this philosophy transnational relations, as opposed to
international relations. After examining and experimenting with
this approach, we have demonstrated the receptiveness of foreign
regions to this idea as well. While developing our Sister City relationship with Vigo, Spain, for example, the Spanish regional government of Galacia approached us to discuss interregional cooperation between Galacia and the entire Virginia Commonwealth.

National governments have political positions that may inter-
fere with co-development. We want to deal with the people of corresponding foreign economic regions without the interference of
politics. We are interested in cross-cultural communication and economic co-development. We want jobs and investment capital and so
do foreign regions. We have found foreign regions whose economic
needs are complementary to ours, and have been successful regardless of differences in the policies of national governments. The techniques that follow are partially grounded in this perspective.

Techniques for international economic development

Export directories   One component of the economic base study
should be a regional industrial directory that lists, at the least, all
the manufacturers, banks, international trade service firms, distributors, and transportation companies in your region. At a minimum, you should have the names of the chief executive officer and
sales manager, number of employees, and a definition of the production activity by Standard Industrial Classification (SIC) code. An
estimate of gross annual sales and an estimate of import activity
and export sales as a percentage of gross also are important. Most
states publish such an industrial directory; to get started, all you
have to do is select companies from your region.

Utilizing the information you have assembled so far, publish an
"export directory" and distribute it to everyone listed in it. A survey
form can be included to update or correct the information and identify interests and needs. Don't be disappointed or discouraged when
you don't get much of a response. Be very careful to note all telephone responses, especially negative ones, from companies that
don't want to be included in what you're doing or don't want information about their company disclosed to others. Be absolutely
sure that your list is inclusive regarding international offices of
banks, freight forwarders, customs-house brokers, and regional export management companies. You want to encourage manufacturers and others to have a choice in selecting services for importing
and exporting. The directory is a marketing tool for trade service
firms. You must treat competitors evenhandedly, so be very careful
not to leave anyone out.

After a reasonable length of time for feedback, so that you are confident that your information is accurate, the export directory becomes one of your primary international marketing tools. You can add industrial site location information or simply use your local industrial site book as a companion marketing piece to the export directory. Once you have targeted the foreign regions you will market to, the information can be translated into the language of your area of interest. Graphics are very important tools for this work, because most people have a strong appreciation for good maps and photographs.

Foreign trade zones   Foreign trade zones (FTZs) are used all around the world. In most other countries, they are known as "free zones." Having a free zone in your area indicates that you are an experienced, sophisticated region with existing international markets. If you don't have one in your region, indicate the nearest and most useful in your export directory and consider starting one in your region.

FTZs have two principal uses. The first is to allow importers to bring goods into the United States through the FTZ and time the payment of duties in accordance with production or distribution processes. The second major use pertains to manufacturing. Companies can bring component parts together, including American-made components, assemble the final product, and reexport it without paying any duties on the foreign components. Both of these uses for free zones are important as assets in international marketing.

Export trading companies   Export trading companies (ETCs) and the techniques involved in using them have not really caught on in the United States yet. Two types of ETCs are in existence. One is industry-specific in that these ETCs group domestic competitors together to establish the international price of one product. The Louisiana Catfish Growers Association is an example of this type of ETC. Typical of the second kind of ETC is the North Dakota group that was founded for the purpose of expanding export sales of the state's agricultural commodities. This type of ETC is not industry-specific or product-specific. The first type of ETC is referred to as "horizontal"; the second, "vertical." Your region may have applications for one or both types of ETC.

Export trading companies have two major problems in the current market. One is that theoretically they are limited to 49 percent import activity and 51 percent export activity by the Export Act of 1982. In the current U.S. market, with a $150 billion trade deficit, this limits the ETC's ability to trade. A second problem is the nation's overall inexperience with countertrade. Countertrade is the technique used by most of the Third World in international transactions.

Under this system, a national government, for example, will require that its purchase of coal be paid for with steel. Estimates are that somewhere between 10 percent and one-third of all international transactions require some countertrade, offset, barter, or buy-back provision. Export trading companies are perfectly designed to answer this problem, but need to be very large to operate in the countertrade environment. So far, only General Electric's ETC and a few others have proven to be effective countertraders—really only because they have to in order to sell their own products.

Gaining experience   With this background, you can see that the formation of ETCs and their effective use require considerable trading experience. In many specific instances, export management companies (EMCs) can handle these situations. The Newport News Export Trading System (NNETS) is a hybrid of the two. NNETS will form ETCs in response to foreign market demand but operates more often through EMCs. The objective is to be able to react to demand. We will bring any combination of trade service firms, including banking, transportation, and export management, together under NNETS to enable the U.S. firm to respond to international demand.

NNETS' orientation toward regional trade development is driven in part by the special nature of our regional economy. As a port city and a rail terminus, we are blessed, both domestically and internationally, with excellent transportation facilities. In identifying an international market that we wish to develop, we strongly consider what we already sell to that foreign market. If we are already supplying this customer, we have a built-in competitive transportation advantage. New products may be price-competitive in that market because of the economies of scale created in the transportation aspect of the export price. For example, we can ship 25 tons of industrial controls to Spain at a lower cost if we are already handling 250 tons of other freight to Spain through our port. This results in lower export prices.

Once a foreign economic region is identified as having corresponding imports and exports—we are selling them something and they are selling us something—and we find ourselves on the same trade route, we seek to broaden that trade. One technique for this is to establish a Sister City relationship with a similar city in that foreign region. This works to build trust, as described earlier. Familiarity with language, customs, culture, and other aspects of the daily life of the foreign region helps build confidence in business relationships. The more different types of cross-cultural communication, the better the relationship. Then the serious work of long-term intraregional co-development can begin. The intimate examination of each other's development needs identifies investment opportunities for them in our market and investment and market opportunities for our companies in their market.

The global perspective and a thorough understanding of your own regional economy, including the transportation aspects of your region, will help to identify additional foreign investment opportunities. We have recently been successful in landing the Canon copier machine factory in Newport News. It will employ at least 1,000 workers and represents one of Japan's largest investments in the United States. (Yes, we have a Sister City in Japan.)

One major reason for the Japanese decision has little to do with even the huge American market for personal copiers. By observing the proper content laws, the Japanese can export these copiers into the European Economic Community (EEC) at an 8.5 percent tariff. If the copiers came from Japan, the EEC tariff would be 100 percent. By being aware of trade relationships like these, you can target your marketing for foreign investments effectively.

Carrying the Canon example one step further enables us to identify certain overseas investment opportunities for U.S. firms. Because the Canon copier, in effect, becomes a U.S. export to the EEC, sales, service, and support for these business machines will be required in Europe. The EEC, however, will likely require that European companies be involved in this business. American dollars can be invested in European companies, or new European companies with U.S. participation can be formed to fulfill this new demand.

New approaches

In conclusion, it must be seen that techniques for local or regional involvement in international economic development require a new and somewhat more sophisticated approach than the typically passive attitudes toward international markets that most Americans have had in the past. Such an approach requires the focused attention of federal, state, and local governments. It has to be a long-term commitment, because it involves a lot of work, organization, trust building, and information.

We believe the regional approach holds the most promise for success. The size, dynamics, and character of a region must be identified and thoroughly understood, and it must be large enough to support the undertaking.

Two characteristics of international economic development make the task much easier. One is that it's fun. Trade development highlights issues and describes the world in a way that everyone enjoys. Other areas of the world are just as interested in getting to know us as we are in knowing them. The other is that it is constantly changing. New trade possibilities are opening up all the time; old ones can change their character almost overnight. There are no static states in the global market. Our ability to handle change with flexibility and responsiveness determines our success.

Getting started need not be expensive. Every region has several economic development organizations. From city development offices to area chambers of commerce—all of whom need to be involved in some way—the contribution of 10 or 20 percent of each organization's overall effort will go a long way toward satisfying direct costs. Networking will provide opportunities for each organization to do what it already does best. No formal regional organization is required until the overall commitment of the various communities in the region is recognized. This is the first requirement for effective international economic development, however. The economic region must be organized, educated, and committed to long-term participation in the global economy.

Today the region, tomorrow the world!

Using Existing Assets to Fund New Development Lending

Paul L. Pryde, Jr.

Cutbacks in federal development assistance have forced many communities to look for alternative ways to finance local economic development projects. This article briefly describes two ways in which cities can use existing, and often underutilized, assets to generate private investment for local job and tax-creating ventures: recycling development loans and funding development deposits with pension assets.

Recycling development loans

One of the principal assets accumulated by many cities over the past 10 years is a portfolio of development loans—loans made with public money to developers, businesses, and individuals in order to create jobs, tax revenues, or housing and business opportunities. To a very large extent, these financial assets, created with community development block grants (CDBGs) and urban development action grants (UDAGs), represent dormant equity, which cities are beginning to use to leverage new private investment for important local projects. Most important, because they are acquired with the proceeds of federal grants rather than local appropriations or bond issues, they impose no cost on local taxpayers. From the standpoint of city administrators, they constitute free money.

According to a report by the Northeast-Midwest Institute, UDAG grants to cities and localities from 1978 through 1982 totaled over $2.3 billion. By the end of 1985, this figure should easily exceed $3 billion. Of the grants made through 1982, Department of Housing and Urban Development (HUD) officials estimate that about 75 percent, or approximately $1.5 billion, have been used by recipient cities to make loans (as opposed to subgrants) to eligible projects. Most of the loans made thus far are reportedly backed by real estate or similar collateral, and many have been made to substantial companies.

Over a somewhat longer period, beginning in 1974, HUD has distributed over $30 billion in CDBG grants to the nation's towns and cities. While CDBG funds are not used solely to make economic development loans, cities have used their CDBG entitlements to finance home improvement loans, building and equipment loans for small business expansion, land acquisition and construction loans for neighborhood improvement projects, and for a number of other purposes. Information on the total volume of loans financed with CDBG funds is not readily available. Nevertheless, it seems reasonable to assume that at least 10 percent of the CDBG funds distributed thus far have been used for economic and community development loans of some description.

There appear to be three types of "secondary use" transactions that cities can employ to make use of what should easily be over $4.5 billion in development assets: loans of development loan repayments, pledges of development loan repayments, and sales of development loans. Brief illustrations of these types of transactions follow.

Loans of development loan repayments Many local economic development projects are too risky to finance entirely with private funds. Incubator facilities are a good example of such a venture. In Fort Wayne, Indiana, where CDBG funds have been used to create a successful home improvement loan program, city officials agreed to lend $325,000 of the interest and principal payments to a local company organized to build an incubator facility for small companies. The city's loan leveraged an additional $1.1 million in private project financing from a major insurance company and local equity investors.

Pledges of development loan repayments The risk associated with local development ventures can often be mitigated by providing lenders guaranties in the form of additional loan collateral. In Chicago, city officials pledged $3 million in repayments from a particularly solid UDAG loan to back tax-exempt bonds issued on behalf of a new manufacturing enterprise.

Sales of development loans Cities often need cash to finance new development loans. In Haverhill, Massachusetts, city officials sold—presumably at a discount to account for the low interest rate on most UDAG loans—a $3 million UDAG loan to Wang Laboratories to the Essex Bank. The loan proceeds are now available to be used to make loans and investments for any economic development project the city sees fit to finance.

Funding development deposits with pension assets

In recent years, banks have responded to the increased volatility in interest rates (and thus in the cost and availability of loanable funds) by shortening the maturities of loans extended to borrowers and adjusting interest rates on these loans at frequent intervals. Small business people who have historically financed their plant and equipment expansion needs with 15-year, fixed-rate loans now face the specter of financing even more expansive capital outlays with 5-year, adjustable-rate debt. The increased risk and cost that borrowers now face can prove a real hindrance to the efforts of a community to expand its small business base. A few areas, however, have begun to exploit a little known provision of federal banking law to attack the small business debt problem. Under current statutes governing deposit insurance, pension funds, unlike other institutional and individual depositors, are permitted to make insured deposits with commercial banks of up to $100,000 per beneficiary. That is to say, while the normal depositor is limited to $100,000 in coverage for its deposits, a pension fund with 10 beneficiaries, for example, can make one insured deposit for $1 million.

In Allegheny County, Pennsylvania, local officials have taken advantage of the special treatment accorded pension assets by creating a special small business financing program. Under the program, the county agrees to make long-term, fixed-rate pension fund deposits with banks that agree to use the funds to make long-term, fixed-rate loans to local small business firms. The Allegheny County program, called the ACTIVE Fund, is an ideal example of the "positive sum" approach to economic development financing, which will increasingly be necessary to involve private lenders and investors in providing capital and credit to local development ventures. Everybody wins.

Because its funds are entirely insured by the Federal Deposit Insurance Corporation (FDIC), the local pension fund is guaranteed a reasonable rate of return on funds used to finance small business without incurring the risk or cost normally associated with small business lending. Local banks are able to make long-term, fixed-rate loans to their small business customers without assuming interest rate risk. Small business borrowers are able to obtain long-term, fixed-rate loans that will enable them to pursue expansion plans safely without the danger of major increases in interest charges. Finally, the county gets the benefits of business expansion, new jobs, and new tax revenues, all of which will improve the job security of the beneficiaries of the pension funds whose deposits are used to finance the program.

Pitfalls in Using Fiscal Impact Analysis

Charles A. Lerable

Local governments, concerned over the cost of development, have come to rely increasingly on a now widely used tool known as fiscal impact analysis to project future costs and revenues associated with a proposed project. While taking a look at how a proposal will affect future city budgets is essential to good city planning, a word of caution is in order: although fiscal impact analysis can be a valuable analytical tool, it is full of potential pitfalls.

In fact, a 1980 study by the U.S. Department of Housing and Urban Development concluded that of the 140 FIAs it reviewed, a majority were considered to be poor quality.[1] This is an alarming statistic because the life or death of a project often hangs on the balance of its fiscal solvency.

Typically, an FIA is undertaken to find out whether the project will pay its own way or which of several project alternatives would be the most fiscally advantageous to a local government. Officials have used the results of FIAs to approve, modify or deny projects. Others have approved projects despite negative fiscal impacts because of overriding social, economic or environmental concern.

In any case, an abundance of development proposals has been shown *not* to pay their own way. For instance, following the passage of Proposition 13, the Governor's Office of Planning and Research [in California] concluded that of the ten residential developments it surveyed, none reported a net fiscal gain.[2] This was a serious statement for a state where many urban areas face a critical shortage of affordable housing.

A number of different methods are used in preparing FIAs, al-

Reprinted with permission from the December 1984 issue of *Western City* magazine, the monthly publication of the League of California Cities.

though typically only two or three types are used, and often in combination:

1. Per capita multiplier. In its simplest form, the per capita method projects the average cost per person of existing services to a project after all nonresidential costs have been removed.
2. Case study. This method projects cost based on the local government's best estimate of service needs for a project.
3. Service standard. This method uses national or regional standards to project average employee and capital costs.

Because FIA is a complicated process, there is the risk of oversimplifying methods, assumptions and conclusions. Perhaps the greatest problem is a general lack of understanding of what FIAs can and cannot do. What follows is a description of some of the common pitfalls in using fiscal impact analysis.

Average versus marginal costing

Average costing assumes the cost to provide services for a new project will equal the existing average cost. (The per capita multiplier uses average costing.) Marginal costing measures the actual cost increment resulting from a project.

Consider one example. An existing fire station fully equipped and staffed is able to serve a geographic area at a fixed cost. New development occurring within the station's service area will have little or no impact on the cost of operating the station; the marginal cost is zero. However, as new development expands outside the service area and a new fire station must be constructed, the marginal cost of serving the new development is equal to the cost of a new fire station. Average costing would attempt to attribute only a portion of the cost of the new station to the development.

In the very long term, average costing generally works. However, marginal costing provides the best gauge of short-term fiscal impacts brought on by the need for new services and capital improvements.

Comparing alternatives

Fiscal impact is the difference between one project and another project or one project compared to a no project alternative. When the question is asked, "What will be the fiscal impact of a project?" the FIA also must address the question, "Compared to what?"

For example, a residential development is proposed to be demolished and a new shopping center constructed in its place. The revenues from the residential development currently exceed costs as will the proposed shopping center. Therefore, the fiscal impact of building the new shopping center is not the $1 million in revenue it will produce, but the $1 million minus the $100,000 the residential development is currently producing.

Changed assumptions, such as inflation and population growth, also can produce considerably different fiscal impacts among proposed projects. For example, one project may show a $100,000 per year positive fiscal impact assuming inflation remains low and population grows rapidly. But a high inflation rate and low population growth may show a $50,000 per year negative fiscal impact for the same project. Therefore, the most useful FIA is one directed at answering the question, "Which of two or more project alternatives has the most positive or least negative fiscal impact based on identical assumptions about the future?"

Assumptions must be validated

Average costing is used extensively in most FIAs. The tendency is to use current service levels and costs in making fiscal projections. However, costs and revenues have remained anything but constant. For instance, since Proposition 13, many local governments have changed their levels of services by either cutting back or slowing growth. These trends should be accounted for in the FIA. Few FIAs quantify the effects that changed assumptions about the future will have on the results, making it difficult for decision makers to foresee the range of fiscal impacts that might actually occur.

Future impacts

The size of the fiscal impact may seem large in comparison to a local government's current budget. A $100,000 per year negative fiscal impact in ten years should not be compared to a $30 million budget today. Rather, the comparison would more likely be made to a $40–50 million dollar budget (using constant dollars) at the time the impact is expected to occur.

Revenues change differently over time

Many FIAs make the assumption that all revenues will rise equally with inflation. They don't. Property, cigarette, gasoline, and motor vehicle in-lieu taxes are examples of revenue sources which do not change directly with inflation.

Fiscal impacts always extend outside the project

The failure to measure outside impacts is perhaps the single greatest shortcoming of many FIAs. The difficulty of analyzing such open-ended impacts probably accounts for this. Yet, unless such impacts are considered, the FIA's validity should be questioned.

A 500-unit residential development may be a fiscal loser if costs and revenues inside the project are considered. However, when the sales tax revenue on the purchases the 500 families will make at a local shopping center outside the project area is included, the project may produce a surplus.

There also is a tendency to balance a residential project with commercial or industrial development to turn a fiscal loser into a fiscal winner. The FIA must address whether this balance already is occurring on an area-wide basis. After all, many cities designate specific areas for residential, commercial or industrial development providing a balance on a citywide rather than project-by-project basis.

Services may decline with revenue

Declining revenue sources should be matched with a projected decline in service. If, for example, citywide gasoline tax revenue is projected to decline after accounting for inflation, there must be a corresponding decline in the level of service, e.g., maintenance. By ignoring predictable declines in service levels but taking into account predictable declines in revenue, FIAs can create false deficits or lower surpluses. The effect of this practice is to project a higher level of service to the project than the city will be financially able to provide elsewhere in the community.

Government officials also should be on the lookout for:

1. Poorly defined assumptions and methodologies which make it impossible to independently duplicate the FIA's results.
2. The generalization that a proposed project will have the same fiscal impact as a similar project in another location.
3. Conclusions directed only at the "bottom line" and which do not analyze the possible effect of changed social, economic and political conditions.
4. FIAs which fail to analyze both the short-term fiscal effects of a phased project and the fiscal effects several years following its completion.

Public officials should be aware of these problems if fiscal impact analysis is to be a useful decision making tool. Thus, an FIA should be prepared only by an experienced staff member or consultant and be subject to a thorough evaluation by an independent second party. The results of the evaluation should be presented jointly with the FIA.

Finally, there is a tendency to overemphasize the easily understood dollars and cents of FIA, i.e., the bottom line. This tendency could overshadow other important economic, social and environmental issues. Using fiscal impact analysis responsibly requires that all issues be addressed on balance with one another.

1.   *The Fiscal Impact Guidebook*, U.S. Dept. of Housing and Urban Development, 1980.

2.   *New Housing: Paying Its Way?*, Office of Planning and Research, 1979.

PART 3

Budgeting Strategies

Public Budgeting Criteria for Assisting Economic Development

George Whelan

While the Center City commuter railroad tunnel is under construction in Philadelphia, the capital program director has developed a feel for when the tunnel is running into a money problem—when the people in the Department of Public Property start getting off the elevator with a cup in hand.

Finance officers are used to the cup-in-hand routine. Pressures build. Trouble is sensed and anticipated. However, exercising sound judgment amid the multiple competing demands for funding is very challenging. Public dollars to assist economic development is a creative area of fiscal policy. Caution is important. This article is an effort to outline criteria for capital budgeting and to some extent for the operating budget with respect to assisting in such situations.

The state of the art with respect to assisting economic development is changing. Land acquisition, writedowns, tax abatement and public improvements were the traditional inducements. Today, the expanded list of tools includes public construction loans, long-term land leases and public funding of front-end costs. Sound fiscal management in this vital area of public policy requires ongoing education to keep pace, and the objective of this article is to assist in developing among public finance officials that educated "feel" as to whether a project is worth supporting and what is an appropriate package of inducements to clinch the private developer's commitment.

Economic and administrative environment

Government entities compete to attract business and industry to enhance and maintain the tax base. In some places there is a decline

Reprinted with permission from the June 1985 issue of *Government Finance Review*.

of the central business district. Some communities face Sun Belt competition. Some are expanding very rapidly; others are growing slowly. In addition, there is a generally acknowledged national shift toward a service economy.

At the same time, public dollars for economic development must vie with demands for municipal buildings, street reconstruction, recreation centers, wage pact settlements, etc. Needless to say, borrowing limits and voter approval also are factors.

Within this context, those in public service can still take a cue from business. We know our communities' strengths. It is possible to devise a strategy to market these strengths. Amid these competing forces, governmental units around the country have an admirable record in attracting business and industry despite the economic uncertainty. Further, public bodies are beginning to assume partnership roles in development ventures. Equity participation in development ventures to minimize the public risk is possible. A community does not have to prostrate itself at the feet of private developers. Mutually beneficial packages can be developed.

A critical administrative prerequisite for assisting economic development with public dollars is the formation of an agreement among the policy makers. The elected officials, the planning commission, township manager and other similar agents form an administrative base. The set of inducements being offered to a private developer has to have broad support to succeed.

The prospect of new tax ratables is the standard compelling factor in the debate over allocating resources. In some localities, an opportunity for citizen involvement in designing a neighborhood shopping center, for example, may be a significant factor. In others, business involvement in and of itself would be a major accomplishment. With the intense competition for the available public resources, an agreement over priorities is vital. Further, the business people want to negotiate with a unified governmental body. Confusion and internal squabbling over the incentive package can adversely affect the deal.

Often there are several governmental and quasi-governmental agencies that have a hand in a project. Aside from the line city departments (e.g., finance, streets and water departments), there may be an urban renewal authority, economic development agency and a business association. Each brings a tool to the venture such as the power of eminent domain, the ability to issue industrial development debt or the influence to schedule complementary privately financed improvements for the development area.

The standard forms of assistance involve arranging zoning, highway access, site improvements, permits, environmental clearances, etc. In large-scale projects, where the list of interested parties and the elements of the development package are very extensive, ongoing interplay among all the participants is as vital as planning and construction progress. In Philadelphia, for example, there are staff task forces representing all the relevant agencies reporting to the mayor's Development Cabinet on a regular basis as the city proceeds with planning its new Convention Center. The Development Cabinet provides a centralized authority for coordination and decision making throughout the process and it serves as the body that evaluates and selects from among competing proposals.

The administrative apparatus is very important. However, there is no substitute for a cadre of experts to marshall the resources in day-to-day management and to evaluate whether a proposal is in the community's best interest. Top-notch people in public service are a very marketable commodity to attract economic development. Business wants to work with able staff, and the taxpayers deserve a thorough scrutiny of the terms of a proposal. Thus, recruiting staff versed in the specifics of development finance and project management as well as in-service training for existing staff would be an investment for any governmental unit. To remain competitive, a governmental unit has to have the players to compete.

Returning to the central concern—public budgeting criteria—the following discussion will examine specific types of development situations and some of the criteria for each instance.

Speculative development situations

A governmental entity can build on speculation with the expectation of attracting new private investment. One might define speculative construction as infrastructure improvements with public dollars to attract new private development. In a manner of speaking, this "venture" capital investment can be recouped from the yield on the eventual tax ratables and by recovering the cost of the land and improvements at the time of the sale.

For example, in Philadelphia, the Penn's Landing project involves an element of speculative construction. By mid-1985, the city and state invested $51.9 million in a 25-acre waterfront property at the foot of Market Street along the Delaware River. The old ferry slip has been dismantled and an embarcadero and boat basin have been constructed. One of the adjacent piers has been enclosed and restored as an indoor tennis complex. The larger plans call for an estimated $200 million in privately developed offices, condominiums, garages, hotel and retail space to be constructed on the site. The dredging, bulkheading and filling at the public's expense literally provide the foundation for the larger complex.

Penn's Landing is also an illustration of an incremental approach designed to limit exposure. Some of the bulkheading was being done in the late 1960s. Pleasure craft began frequenting the marina around the time of the Bicentennial. A large public area has been used for a variety of festivals in recent years. The large-scale private development is being planned and a number of developers have been approached by the city in that regard. Clearly, it has taken time. As a result, the expense has not been concentrated so as to be overly burdensome in any given year.

The key criterion is a judgment as to the eventual marketability of the site once the improvements are complete. Many localities have seemingly useless parcels of ground in otherwise attractive locations where some public investment would produce some long-term rewards. Penn's Landing was nothing more than a muddy river bank. Consultations with the local real estate community can be valuable in assessing such opportunities.

There has been some discussion about using the tax incremental financing (TIF) technique in connection with Penn's Landing and some adjacent waterfront parcels. The tax yield from the expected ratables would be pledged to retire the debt. The hiatus period between the public improvements and the eventual private development described above makes TIF unsuitable for financing this type of undertaking. In speculative situations, the time lag would generally be too long to make tax incremental financing useful, but the incremental financing technique may be suitable in other situations.

Another speculative situation involves a rather simple method for developing industrial parks. The Interport Complex in Philadelphia involves a large tract of land being developed into an industrial park. Converting tracts of land to industrial parks is common, but there are still costs and risks. One means to evaluate opportunities is a requirement to recover the up-front public costs at the time of the land sale. Capitalizing the cost of all the initial land acquisition, site preparation, streets and water and sewer lines in the price of each parcel at the time of sale is a basis for a revolving fund. The initial amount of money for developing the tract of land was provided by a bond issue. The sales receipts were then "recycled" and used to prepare each new tract sector. Again, the incremental and self-sustaining approach offers some comfort to limit the public body's exposure. Actually, if all the sunk costs are recovered at the time of sale, the eventual tax yields from the new ratable are a free and clear return on investment. In some instances, selling the parcels with a write-down might still be worthwhile, given the long-term tax yields. Again, the potential market for the land tract must be carefully assessed before embarking on such an undertaking.

One final venturesome idea requires a great deal of caution. Construction of a specific type of facility on speculation for a particular kind of enterprise operation is proposed occasionally as a necessary marketing step in the intensely competitive environment. For example, a certain type of port facility for a shipping company, a warehouse along a new section of an interstate highway, or a new terminal for an airport operation might be suggested as surefire public investments. If these facilities were in place, the proponents argue, there is a strong likelihood revenues from likely future operators would be sufficient to retire the debt.

A long-term operator's lease guaranteeing sufficient revenues to retire the debt should be a requirement to begin such a project. One approach could be initial public improvements, such as access roads, to establish the good faith interest of the local government in the overall strategy. Large-scale construction for hypothetical private operators involves a considerable amount of risk and ought to be approached with skepticism. As with all the preceding examples, assessing the potential demand is the heart of the risk/reward equation decision.

Customized inducements

In the process of negotiating development commitments, the set of public contributions or inducements can be termed a customized package. The basic forms of assistance may not be unique; however, the particular mixture and magnitude of the public incentives can vary from project to project.

Will a new public parking lot seal the agreement? Are density bonuses for certain amenities and design features necessary? Should the city buy the land and lease it to the developer? Should the city or the developer be responsible for the public area in the new commercial complex? These are the kinds of questions that surface as plans and commitments are finalized.

The first step for local government officials is an evaluation of the basic proposal. This involves gauging the potential demand for the proposed retail, office or commercial space. Is there a persuasive market analysis? Is there any potential for public use or joint use? Is there an agreement among local officials to support that particular type of proposed development? Is the site the best? Are there other sites? What are the estimated tax yields and job creation effects?

Is the proposed design acceptable? Does the design provide enough in the way of public amenities? Are the cost estimates and financial pro forma analyses reasonable? Does the developer have construction financing, permanent financing and tenant commitments? What is the financial condition of the developer?[1] Intertwined in this matrix of questions is the possibility of inducements or contributions on the part of the public entity. For example, if space is needed for governmental offices, agreeing to become a tenant can help the developer obtain bank commitments.

Governmental entities need to understand the constraints faced by the private development industry. In large-scale redevelopment projects, the front-end investment capital is a major constraint for the entrepreneur. Specifically, the acquisition of land, relocation costs, air rights, clearance, utilities and other basic public site improvements are substantial considerations affecting the ultimate cash flow scenarios. In addition, the time it takes the public sector to make decisions and provide all the necessary regulatory approvals such as building permits, environmental clearances and zoning can be a significant obstacle.[2]

The complexity and size of renewal efforts have led to a partnership approach between the public and private parties in many instances. Both parties accept a degree of risk as decisions are made on questions of which party pays for which element of the overall project. The partnership approach enables public officials to act as packagers and expediters for the venture. Up-front costs are a significant obstacle for developers. Therein lies a particular opportunity for public inducements. The land could be acquired through eminent domain, for example, and leased or sold at a reduced price to the developer. That initial outlay would be removed from the developer's calculations. In exchange, communities could insist on equity "kickers" as part of the land lease to reduce the public risk; e.g., a percentage of the net revenue after five years of operation. Principal payments also could be deferred to assist with initial cash flow. Or, the whole range of up-front expenses, including planning and relocation costs, could be borne by the governmental body. Aside from reducing costs, that is a way to ensure design control. To describe these methods in concrete terms, a particular example from Philadelphia can be used as an illustration.

Gallery I opened in Center City Philadelphia in 1977. It is a three-story shopping mall anchored on one end by a renovated department store and at the other end by a new department store with 125 retail stores filling out the balance of the mall. Gallery II extends the overall space with an additional 170,000 square foot shopping mall (again three stories) and a new 180,000 square foot department store. A 450,000 square foot office building and a 750-car garage are located on an adjacent land parcel.

A number of noteworthy incentive techniques are involved in the Gallery II project. The Redevelopment Authority of the City of Philadelphia leased the lot to the Gallery II developer for 99 years in return for some profit participation. Lease payments are at a set rate for the first five years. In years six through 35 the lease payment is the greater amount of $1.45 per square foot or 7½ percent of net cash flow less operating expenses and debt service. This kind of participation is an illustration of a public landholder waiving payments for land in return for some participation. As a result, the developer does not have a substantial land acquisition expense up front. At the same time the city has a return on its investment. It should be noted that the acquisition was in part paid from the city's capital budget. In total, $17 million of general obligation funds went into Gallery II for acquisition, relocation, demolition and design.

Another public incentive is the maintenance agreement for both Gallery I and II. The common area of the Gallery is maintained by a mall maintenance corporation with the city contributing 50 percent or an amount determined by a specified formula for support of that corporation. There is a cap on the city's obligation in future years. The cost of this is estimated to be in excess of $1.5 million for fiscal year 1984. The mall area is a vital public concern because it connects with the waiting area for a major rail transit hub.

Yet another feature of the Gallery II package is the use of Community Development Block Grant (CDBG) monies as a construction loan float. The federal block grant each year involves a letter of credit in connection with each grant awarded. The cash is drawn down, essentially on a voucher basis, for the various community development projects. The regulations permit the cash to be drawn down well in advance of actual need for certain purposes. Consequently, a float can be created, as in the case of Gallery II.

One of the department stores in the complex paid the Redevelopment Authority to construct a store shell in Gallery II. Additionally, a long-term lease, such as described above, was arranged. The CDBG float in effect was used as an interest-free construction loan. The $2 million estimated savings was clearly a benefit and an incentive for the firm. It should also be noted that the CDBG float was backed by a letter of credit to ensure the city would be repaid.

The city also has a substantial commitment to encourage minority businesses in Gallery II. Again using CDBG dollars, the Philadelphia City-Wide Development Corporation provides 3 percent seven-year loans as equity dollars to minority entrepreneurs to enable them to obtain commercial loans. Further, the interest payments on the commercial loans are subsidized up to 30 percent. Only the principal amount of the subsidy has to be repaid at the end of seven years.

Another tactic to foster economic development involves the adjacent One Reading Center office building and parking garage. The city leases 200,000 square feet of the total 720,000 square feet of office space for a term of 25 years in One Reading Center. The estimated cost of this is $5.6 million per year. The city can "shrink" its space commitment if commercial demand for space dictates. Under a rent incentive plan the city receives a portion of the net operating income in excess of the base amount. Again, the city wanted some participation in return for such a commitment. The debt service of the industrial development bonds connected with the parking garage is guaranteed by the city. The potential exposure to the general fund of honoring that guarantee was weighed against the benefit of helping to cement the entire package. In the process, a $19 million Urban Development Action Grant (UDAG) and a $3.3 million Economic Development Administration (EDA) grant were obtained for the entire project. Needless to say, this is a complicated case study of public and private partnership.

A principal measurement of this project's value is the tax yields. It is estimated that one department store alone will generate $1.5 million in local taxes per year for the next 20 years. One Reading Center is expected to generate $3.6 million in local tax revenue. The parking garage is expected to generate another $400,000 on an annual basis. The particulars were hammered out with an eye to the developer's cash flow and return on equity while also looking at the ultimate return for the City of Philadelphia. The prospective tax yields alone were not sufficient. The equity participation in return for assuming some front-end costs is a special facet of this experience.

To illustrate another locality's method for gauging its return on investment, an excerpt from the St. Paul, Minnesota, capital allocation policy is shown in Exhibit 1. Note the specific thresholds of return that must be met to justify public expenditures.

It is critical to emphasize the equity contribution of federal and state agencies in economic development ventures such as the Gallery and One Reading Center Complex. There is a long-standing role of government to assume an avant-garde role in areas of critical need.[3] The leveraging effect of UDAG or EDA grants around the country has been crucial to attract investment in renewal areas. It reduces the exposure for all. In a similar vein, major street restorations, new intersections adjacent to new hotels or office complexes, renovated mass transit stations and other strategic public improvements can be accelerated or concentrated to coincide with private development. Aggressively seeking intergovernmental grants for these special improvements eases the local burdens. State and federal people in all agencies are very receptive to leveraging their grant monies. Actually, when a developer assesses opportunities in various communities a major criterion is the ability of the community's officials to orchestrate all these instruments in a timely fashion to complement the private effort.

Many jurisdictions assist renewal efforts on a much smaller scale. Commercial strips in older residential neighborhoods are usually comprised of small businesses. Often they have declined as the metropolitan areas have expanded. The city or town can accelerate street improvement schedules to coincide with small business loans. Do the businesses make their improvements first? Who pays for the new overhead veranda, the new trees and trash receptacles? Why can't the city increase the number of police foot patrols on Friday evenings?

The proprietors need to see some good faith efforts on the part

Exhibit 1. Economic development policies.

Policy K

Allocation of capital funds for economic development proposals will be based on the merits of each proposal and upon its ability to leverage private investment dollars and obtain a return of increased property taxes in accordance with the identified leverage and return of investment guidelines.

1. **Leverage guidelines:** Normal leveraging is 1:6. In other words, each dollar the city provides for a particular project should mean six capital dollars committed by the developer. For example, the city could normally anticipate providing no more than $60,000 in public improvements to service systems or in subsidy to a project valued at $360,000.

   This ratio may go as low as 1:3 if a given project will have a major impact on a public goal. Examples of such potentially worthwhile projects include:

   a. Projects directly associated with neighborhood revitalization efforts;
   b. Projects which generate additional (not displacement) employment within Saint Paul; and
   c. Projects whose principal objective is resource conservation or the development of alternate energy sources.

2. **Return on investment guidelines:** Normal return on investments is 12 percent. In other words, the city expects to realize a direct return of 12 percent property taxes for its participation in an economic development project. If $75,000 in public improvements are provided, tax receipts from the project should be $9,000 per year more than they were before development.

   This return on investment may go as low as 4 percent if a given project will have a major impact on a public goal. Examples of such potentially worthwhile projects are given in 1, above.

   However, at a minimum, the tax yield from a project should cover the cost of any additional municipal services required.

Policy L

Tax abatement is discouraged as a development incentive. However, it may be used to support projects that explicitly serve a public purpose. If used, abated valuation in any year of the abatement period must not be lower than the valuation of land and improvements before the project is started, increased at a 6 percent rate compounded annually over the term of abatement.

Sources: *Saint Paul Capital Allocation Policy 1979, 1980, 1981;* Council for Urban Economic Development, *A Case Study Analysis, Development Financing,* p. 62.

of the governmental bodies before replacing windows, buying new awnings and investing in new inventories. For the public body, special assessments, sharing costs for some of the street restoration, and intergovernmental grants can reduce costs. A lot of meetings and some timely public action to fulfill promises can catalyze the local businesses into responding in kind with their own investments to rejuvenate.

Social benefits

The thrust of the criteria thus far has been measured in tax yields, equity participation and similar financial indicators. Social benefits also fit into the matrix of evaluation criteria. Job creation is a classic benefit. An appropriate question to a developer would be how many construction jobs and how many permanent jobs will be created? Fostering minority and female entrepreneurial opportunities by establishing goals for tenant occupancy in a commercial venture is another example. The Gallery II minority business efforts are a clear illustration of this approach. Similar goals for employment during construction also might be utilized.

Citizen participation in project planning can yield benefits in later years in the form of increased patronage of the new facility as well as the intangible quality of increased civic pride. Community support can help obtain approval from elected officials. The absence of it can be problematic.

Conclusion

The traditional role of the finance officer is applicable in this area of economic development. The finance officer has always been a guardian of the public purse. The old dictum of *caveat emptor* applies to the finance officer's responsibility in the process. Will the speculative infrastructure improvements ultimately lead to a commitment from a hotel developer? Is guaranteeing debt service vital in order to seal an agreement and is it worth the exposure to the general fund? Does a deal involve too much subsidy? Studying the developers' pro forma analysis to determine an appropriate return on equity is not an inappropriate exercise. Economic development is only one demand on the community's financial resources. There are many other demands.

The economic development people, the private interests and, at times, the elected officials all have a bias to close the deal. That is their responsibility. However, the obligation to take a hard look at the numbers rests squarely on the finance department's shoulders, as well it should.

This article began by describing a hunch as part of decision making. After running and re-running the numbers and asking the questions, a good sense of the proposal is the goal. To reach that point requires expertise and an effort to keep informed about economic development techniques. One is never certain about big decisions. However, thorough analyses can create that intuitive picture about the correctness of a decision.

1. Urban Land Institute, *Downtown Development Handbook*, Community Builders Handbook Series (Washington, D.C.: Urban Land Institute, 1980), Chapter 4, 5 and 6.
2. National Council for Urban Economic Development, *Coordinated Urban Economic Development: A Case Study Analysis, Development Financing* (National Council for Urban Economic Development: Washington, D.C., 1978), pp. 1–3.
3. Otto Eckstein, *Public Finance* (Englewood Cliffs, N.J.: Princeton-Hall, Inc., 1979), pp. 8–9.

Bibliography

American Planning Association. *Local Capital Improvements and Development Management, Analysis and Case Studies.* American Planning Association: Chicago, Ill., 1980.

Moak, Lennox L., and Killian, Kathryn W. *Capital Programming and Capital Budgeting.* Municipal Finance Officers Association: Chicago, Ill., 1964.

National Council for Urban Economic Development. *Development Financing,* Coordinated Urban Economic Development Series. National Council for Urban Economic Development: Washington, D.C., 1978.

Philadelphia City Planning Commission. *Issues for the 1980's.* Philadelphia City Planning Commission, Philadelphia, Pa.

Urban Land Institute. *Downtown Development Handbook,* Community Builders Handbook Series. Urban Land Institute: Washington, D.C., 1980.

Material and information provided by the Philadelphia Industrial Development Corporation, Market Street East Development Corporation and the Philadelphia City Planning Commission.

Budgeting for State and Local Infrastructure

John M. Kamensky

Doomsayers have been harkening the "disinvestment" of America's public infrastructure for several years in the popular press. They advocate more capital spending to reverse the effects of investment trends which have been declining (in constant dollars) since the late 1960s. Estimates for reversing these trends are as high as $3 trillion (about the size of current GNP) between now and 2002. Roger Vaughn of the Gallatin Institute points out that to do this, state and local taxes would have to increase by 40 percent.[1] This is obviously impossible. So where do we begin?

This article suggests that current analyses of infrastructure trends have not adequately accounted for several factors which influence the supply and demand for public capital. These factors, in some cases, are disincentives to further investment. However, the objective of policy makers should not necessarily be to resume the investment growth trends of the past. By clearly identifying and assessing certain supply and demand factors, the reasons for "disinvesting" become clearer. With this understanding, several principles can be established which, in turn, serve as useful guides in developing a strategy for budgeting for state and local capital investment.

What is public infrastructure?

"Public infrastructure" is a catchall phrase. No consistent definition exists. Some use it to encompass all governmental capital investment, including social investment such as education and health care.[2] Most define public infrastructure as investment in the con-

Reprinted with permission from the Autumn 1984 issue of *Public Budgeting & Finance*.

struction, repair, and maintenance of fixed, physical assets.[3] This analysis uses a more restrictive definition, developed by the U.S. Bureau of Economic Analysis (BEA), which defines it as capital outlays for new construction put in place and associated capital equipment outlays.[4] This excludes maintenance and repair expenditures which cannot be clearly distinguished when allocated between operating and capital budgets via existing governmental accounting procedures. In addition, this analysis also excludes direct federal investment (such as post offices and military installations) and government-owned housing. It focuses on state and local fixed-capital investments which, however, may be financed in part or wholly by federal grants-in-aid.

Trends in public infrastructure: existing stock and new investment

The value of existing state and local capital stock already in place has increased 15-fold since 1950. The average growth rate was 9 percent per year. However, the 1980–82 period shows an annual growth of only 1.4 percent. This significant change in the rate of growth is related to the steady decline of new annual investment (in constant 1972 dollars) since 1968.[5]

The estimated current value of existing state and local capital stock in place in 1982 was $2.1 trillion. Highways, streets, and bridges are the largest category, comprising 39 percent of the total, with education buildings coming in second with 20 percent of the total. Highways tend to be primarily a state responsibility while education buildings tend to be chiefly a local government responsibility.

The growth in state and local capital stock since 1950 has been rapid, but when the effects of inflation and depreciation are considered, a different picture emerges. While the value of capital stock increased at an annual rate of 9 percent since 1950, the constant dollar measure shows a much lower rate of 3.8 percent. Since 1970, constant dollar stock trends have grown at an average annual rate of 2.6 percent. However, when growth is measured net of depreciation, the value of existing stock increased only 0.1 percent between 1981 and 1982.

The slow growth during the 1970s and the stagnant trend of the early 1980s is not occurring in all categories of infrastructure. When the growth trends of each of the functional components of state and local capital (in constant dollars, net of depreciation) are disaggregated, we find that two categories—highways and education buildings—are the biggest influences on overall capital stock trends because of their disproportionate share of total infrastructure. The slower growth trends of highways and education, as will be discussed later, are due to a decline in the demand for education facilities and the approaching completion of the interstate highway system.

In constant dollars, annual investment outlays peaked in 1968 at $35.9 billion and have declined ever since. Investment in 1982 was $21.1 billion. When the constant dollar trends are disaggregated into functional categories, rates of growth and change are less stable for annual investment trends than for annual stock trends. In the late 1970s, though, annual investment in infrastructure decreased or became stagnant for nearly every major category of infrastructure.

By discounting the effects of highway and education investment, a more stable trend is evident. Nevertheless, other categories of infrastructure began to decline in the late 1970s, paralleling the capital stock trends.

An important relationship between the stagnant growth trends of capital stock discussed earlier and the annual investment trends is that annual investment is not keeping pace with the depreciation of capital stock. As annual investment declines, the average age of existing stock increases. As a result, the effects of depreciation on the value of existing stock increase.

Depreciation of existing stock may soon exceed annual new investment trends. Because new investment is not keeping up with inflation or depreciation, inadequate or obsolete infrastructure remains unreplaced. This is in sharp contrast to the growth of private sector capital investment during the past decade.

Another factor in annual investment, which has not been considered in the above analysis because of lack of data, is the adequacy of the amounts spent on maintenance and repair of existing facilities. The investment trends are based on expenditures for new capital only; however, anecdotal information seems to suggest similar trends for maintenance and repair.[6] While national figures cannot be compiled because of the variations in state and local accounting techniques, this facet in the annual investment equation cannot be overlooked by those financing and delivering the services.

Several researchers believe that public works investment is a prerequisite to continued private sector expansion.[7] If public sector infrastructure is inadequate, it is argued, private sector growth could be stifled. By citing the graphic downward trends in capital stock and annual investment, many policy makers have concluded that a crisis exists and more money needs to be spent to reverse this trend. This conventional (and superficial) conclusion and response requires deeper review because it is important to understand why "disinvestment" is occurring.[8] Understanding this will help develop several guiding principles which may assist states and localities in budgeting more wisely for their infrastructure needs.

Why has new investment stagnated?

A complex web of developments spawned during the past two decades has contributed to the steady decline in new investment in state and local infrastructure. Many of these developments stem from radical changes in the way this investment is financed. These changes, in turn, have often discouraged state and local investment; conversely, in other instances they may have fostered an artificial demand for facilities. A second set of developments stems from important changes in the demand for new capital facilities.

The combined effect of these two developments influences the capital stock and annual investment trends discussed above. When these changes in supply and demand are fully considered, it becomes less clear whether concerted efforts should be made to reverse the declining investment trends for public infrastructure. Clearly, as will be discussed later, some selective response is appropriate to reduce existing disincentives to invest, but the objective of policy making should not be, as some suggest, to "catch up" and resume the state and local investment trends of the 1960s.

Changes in infrastructure financing   State and local infrastructure has traditionally relied on three sources of finance: federal aid, municipal bonds, and own-source current revenues (taxes, fees, etc.). Federal aid as a source of financing increased dramatically over the past decade, paying for 24 percent of state and local infrastructure in 1970 and peaking at 44 percent in 1979. The municipal bond market also grew dramatically during this period (in constant dollars), but, as will be seen, a decreasing share of that market was used for infrastructure. Own-source current revenues tend to be cyclical sources of capital investment and are heavily influenced by the conditions of state and local operating budgets.

The significant shifts that have occurred among these sources of finance have altered an array of state and local investment. Larry Hush, an economist with the U.S. Office of Management and Budget, suggests that increased federal aid is responsible for the overall decline in new investment. He points out that states and localities cut back their non-education capital spending by $2.40 for every $1.00 increase in federal capital grants since 1970. He concludes: "Further expansion of the federal role may merely result in even greater reductions by states and localities, resulting in net declines in total real capital spending."[9]

While increased federal aid may contribute to the phenomenon of state and localities substituting federal dollars for their own spending on capital projects, another associated phenomenon may be even more significant in explaining why states and localities have reduced investment in their own infrastructure. Hush sug-

gests that states and localities expect that the federal government
will continue to finance a growing portion of their infrastructure.
This "expectation" deters state and local investment because they
are waiting for "their turn" in the long line of federal aid recipients.
They perceive that a wait of several years is more beneficial than
committing themselves to repaying a 20- or 30-year bond. This is a
fundamental change in state and local perceptions of their roles and
responsibilities for specific categories of infrastructure. This increased dependency on federal aid has occurred in other areas of
intergovernmental finance over the past two decades, not just in the
area of infrastructure. This growth and attendant change in perceptions has been carefully documented in a series of studies by the
U.S. Advisory Commission on Intergovernmental Relations.[10] The
displacement effect of federal capital aid, however, seems to be
greater than for other forms of federal aid because capital projects
are more easily postponed.[11]

As the federal role in infrastructure finance increased during
the 1970s, the role of municipal bonds decreased from its traditional
share of 50 percent of state and local infrastructure financing to a
low of 29 percent in 1981. While the role of municipal bonds decreased, the bond market itself did not. The market refocused its
role away from financing public infrastructure to the financing of
private ventures. In 1970, 95 percent of bonds were used to finance
traditional infrastructure. By 1982, only 45 percent of new long-
term bonds were used to finance infrastructure. This shift has resulted in increased market volume which, bond analysts say, increases competition for capital. This, in turn, increases overall
interest costs in the market, including costs to borrowers for public
capital.[12] Other changes in the structure of the market have also
contributed to increased interest costs.[13] These factors have resulted in higher state and local debt servicing costs, meaning more
must be spent to finance debt and less is available for capital investment. For instance, in 1970 about 21 percent of total debt service
went to interest payments; in 1980, 37 percent went to interest payments.

The use of state and local current revenue sources to finance
debt varies. While some jurisdictions face severe restrictions when
borrowing for capital projects and must resort to current revenues,
most rely on current revenues in a cyclical pattern.[14] As a result, the
allocation of current revenues for infrastructure must compete with
operating budget needs.

As a secondary effect of the increased federal role in intergovernmental relations, state and local priorities shifted from economic capital to social, or consumption, expenditures.[15] In many
cases this shift was prodded by federal "seed" grants which created
constituency groups that demanded state and local funding after

the federal grant ended. As a result, when current revenue resources stopped growing, budget choices were made between operating budgets and capital budgets. Invariably, operating budgets won
out. This competition was exacerbated in recent years when budgets
were reduced because of tax revolts, poor fiscal conditions, and reduced federal aid. Many observers note that the typical result was
deferred capital spending from current revenue sources.[16]

So, a combination of factors have led to changes in the ways
infrastructure has been traditionally financed. These changes, dom-
inated primarily by the increased federal role, have weakened state
and local incentives to bear the responsibility for infrastructure investment and have contributed to reallocating the uses of bonds and
current revenues to other endeavors. However, this is only one side
of the explanation for state and local reductions in infrastructure
investment.

Changes in demand for infrastructure investment In addition to changes in the financing of infrastructure which adversely
affected state and local investment incentives, important changes in
the demand for services have also contributed to a reduction in new
investment. Many analysts have not adequately addressed these
changes when projecting infrastructure financing needs; they may
be, therefore, overestimating actual needs. While growth is occurring in some areas of the country, thereby stimulating new demand,
significant declines in demand are occurring in other areas of the
country or in specific categories of infrastructure, which suggests
that the aggregate decline in investment trends may be altogether
appropriate.

These changes are due to factors such as demographic shifts,
the use of better pricing mechanisms (which reduce demand), and
changes in the way services are delivered, such as shifts of responsibility for specific capital facilities from the public to the private
sectors. Additionally, George Peterson of the Urban Institute has
proposed that we rethink the standards by which "need" is measured. This too could contribute significantly to reduced demand for
infrastructure.

The most significant demographic shift affecting one category
of infrastructure, education buildings, is the post-baby boom decline in the school age population during the 1970s.[17] Fewer students
translate into reduced investment demands, and as school district
sell off surplus buildings, the value of infrastructure stock declines.
Other demographic changes include population growth in southern
and western regions, decline in the Northeast, and movement from
urban to non-urban areas. These shifts reallocate infrastructure demands with growing areas requiring new construction and declining areas needing maintenance and repair of aging structures. The

aggregate effect of demographic shifts on demand, however, is unclear because of inadequate data.

Expanded reliance on user fees to finance capital development can, in theory, contribute to lower levels of demand for infrastructure. A growing number of indicators point to increased use of fees to finance infrastructure.[18] Analysts, however, have not attempted to assess the effects of this trend vis-a-vis the trend of reduced investment in infrastructure.

A third trend is the privatization of certain categories of infrastructure. Historically the responsibility for meeting certain public needs has shifted from one sector of the economy to the other. For instance, in the nation's early days, many highways and canals were privately owned. Over time they became a public responsibility.[19] Also in different regions of the country, public and private responsibilities differ. Utilities in some areas of the country are publicly owned; in others, they are private.

Currently there is a trend toward privatizing capital facilities.[20] As the private sector buys existing government facilities or makes a direct investment, the value of public stock and public investment falls. This is clearly happening in hospital construction and is occurring to a greater degree in the areas of streets, and water and sewer lines.[21] Therefore, any analysis of declining public investment must taken into account this shift before "needs" are projected. Unfortunately, good data on these trends are not available.

Finally, construction standards contribute significantly to what is perceived as the level of demand for capital investment. George Peterson points out: "Capital standards are not 'needs' in any literal sense, but are merely policy objectives which must be balanced against their costs of achievement."[22]

When examined in the aggregate, changes in demand suggest that efforts to reverse declining investment trends may not be an appropriate objective. More careful analyses are needed before resource allocation goals are established, but this should not be a reason to delay decisions to act. There are identified infrastructure problems which have demonstrable adverse effects. However, the calls for a massive investment campaign need to be tempered with an understanding of the causes of declining investment.

The effects of declining public investment

The Congressional Budget Office (CBO) identified three converging sets of problems related to declining investments in infrastructure: deterioration, technological obsolescence, and insufficient capacity to serve future growth.[23] In addition the press is full of anecdotal instances of the effects of the deterioration of infrastructure stemming from declining investment.[24] CBO has summarized these adverse effects as:

1. Higher costs borne by users of inadequate or deteriorated facilities
2. Higher life-cycle construction costs for facilities which are not properly maintained
3. Potentially significant constraints on economic development.[25]

For example, inadequate airports create congestion and delay. This cost the airlines $1 billion in 1980, wasted 700 million gallons of fuel, and resulted in 60 million hours of waiting time for passengers. Expanded airport capacity could help correct this problem. In the case of life-cycle costs, deferred bridge deck maintenance quickly leads to the need to replace the deck.[26] Individual examples such as these can be quantified; however, they do not lend themselves to an easy aggregation of national costs.

In the case of economic development, effects are even more elusive. While Choate claims that one-half to two-thirds of the nation's communities are unable to support economic development until major new investments are made in basic facilities such as wastewater treatment plants,[27] Peterson says the actual reliance of business on public infrastructure has not been adequately researched: "At present we know next to nothing about the use of public capital facilities by business firms of various industrial classifications," and "until these basic pieces of the business-and-infrastructure puzzle are put together, we will be unable to go beyond unsupported (and often extreme) speculation about the role of capital in the next generation of industrial modernization."[28] The determinants of the aggregate effects of infrastructure investment (or the lack thereof), however, are as hazy as attempts to assess aggregate levels of need.

Determining investment needs

Infrastructure needs of state and local governments are really value judgments rather than accepted measures, and projections of needs reveal the implications of a set of values, not the probable future. CBO notes that, since need is conditioned by desired quality and the level of demand, no single definition of need can be developed for state and local infrastructure investment.[29] Need varies by functional category as well as by geographic region. Decisions, therefore, must be made in the context of individual components. This, however, has not been the case in recent analyses of infrastructure needs.

In general, three approaches have been used to determine infrastructure needs. One approach has been to project historical growth trends into the future and compare this with a projection of current investment patterns. The resulting "gap" between the two trends is the additional investment required. The second approach estimates the costs of maintaining existing levels of service by investing enough to stem further physical deterioration. The third approach estimates needs based on uniform standards such as those prescribed by federal law.

The Morgan Guaranty Trust Co. estimated investment needs based on historical versus current spending trends. It found that spending on state and local infrastructure (adjusted to account for the rise and fall in education and highway spending) rose at an average annual rate of 2.4 percent between 1950 and 1980. In recent years, however, the average annual increase was only 0.7 percent. The resulting "gap" in spending, by 1985, would be $182 billion in constant dollars, or $500 billion in current dollars.[30] This method, of course, assumes historical growth trends and constant levels of demand, and does not account for shifts of infrastructure responsibilities between the public and private sectors.

The Urban Institute has compiled some infrastructure cost data from federal studies of expenditures necessary to maintain current levels of service in four functional categories (highways, bridges, mass transit, and sewers). The total is $536.7 billion.[31] The Associated General Contractors of America expanded this list to include other items and estimates existing needs at $905 billion.[32] Combining both existing and future needs, based on federal standards, CBO sees a need to spend $53.4 billion a year in seven functional categories, and the Associated General Contractors estimates an aggregate cost of $3.03 trillion by 2002.[33]

The advantage of these studies over the Morgan Guaranty trend projection is that they can compensate for changes in demand, can capture replacement costs, and can account for changes in quality and standards over time. Each of these factors, however, is merely a reflection of a set of values and cannot be taken as an objective need.

While a number of analysts suggest major, concerted efforts at all levels of government to "fill the gap" created by declining annual investments over the past decade, the Department of Commerce concludes, in its *1983 U.S. Industrial Outlook*:

Even assuming no major public policy changes, the long-term decline in public construction will probably end during the next five years. The underlying need for public construction is strong, and the ability of governments to pay for it should improve as a result of economic growth, declining interest rates, and growing public recognition of the deteriorating condition of the stock of public works.[34]

A third approach to assessing needs is to base them on existing standards. However, these are implicit sets of values and should not be thought of as immutable. George Peterson says: "Although need gaps are usually thought to be filled by additional spending, they also can be closed by reconsidering and reducing the needs standards that have given rise to the investment gap."[35] In other words, policy objectives need to be balanced with potential costs.

Need, therefore, must be analyzed in relation to costs; however, it should also be analyzed in relation to anticipated demand levels. The existing studies of infrastructure needs spend much effort on attempting to quantify costs but do not adequately assess changes in levels of demand. Vaughn warns of dramatic structural changes in the economy during the upcoming decade which will lead to significant shifts in demand for different kinds of public capital investment.[36] He highlights potential changes in areas such as technological innovation, demographic trends, the effects of world trade, and management of limited natural resources.

These unknown demand trends suggest that the goals should not be to resume old infrastructure investment trends. Even projected trends are hazardous. Therefore, there is a need to develop a flexible, forward-looking investment strategy. Instead of setting spending goals, there is need for a set of investment principles. If properly structured, the competing forces of supply and demand will allocate investment resources within that framework.

Developing an investment strategy

A sensible approach to structuring an investment strategy is to establish a set of principles incorporating both the supply and demand aspects of infrastructure and to use both as guides in making capital decisions. The objective of such a strategy should not be to change the existing investment trends by committing the public sector to target dollar investment objectives. Rather, it should seek to improve infrastructure by changing the existing set of investment disincentives. The following principles seek to do this.

Accountability and responsibility levels should be defined

The significant changes in infrastructure financing over the past two decades have substantially altered the roles of federal, state and local government responsibilities for constructing and maintaining infrastructure. The resulting diffusion of responsibilities has created institutional obstacles and slowed the decision-making process. The federal record of its involvement, as documented by the ACIR, has been one of poor accountability and inadequate implementation. The ACIR calls for a sorting out of responsibility and the protection of state and local autonomy.[37] The ad hoc federal role in infrastructure policy making interferes with the traditionally decentralized, diverse nature of the decision-making structures in place prior to the expanded level of federal involvement. CBO developed a set of criteria which it believes should govern federal involvement in future infrastructure investments.[38] These include cases where:

1. Costs and benefits of public activities flow across state borders
2. Centralized planning and management are needed to improve economic efficiency and ensure a coordinated national network
3. Need dictates sharing national resources with distressed regions or areas of the country.

A defined, limited federal role will clarify responsibilities and reduce instances of delayed state and local investment decisions which stem from expectations that the federal government will finance investments.

Investment decisions should be based on individual components of infrastructure The severity, scope, and specific characteristics of infrastructure problems differ widely between and within the various categories.[39] In some parts of the country, roads need to be built; in other parts, they need to be repaired. As a result, no all-encompassing program or specific dollar targets can or should be developed for infrastructure. Such an approach would be wasteful ("the dollars are there, so let's spend them"). A more efficient approach is to base investment decisions on an aggregate of individual projects, not on abstract needs.[40] But how should investment decisions on individual projects be made?

A project should be based on future needs, not past trends Investment decisions should anticipate changing future demand and not be based on past trends. For instance, should a county build a needed hospital or, because hospitals are increasingly being privatized, should the county instead encourage private sector action? Vaughn identifies four areas which should be considered when assessing the demand for future public infrastructure.[41]

1. Changing demographics. Shifts in the age of the population and its geographic distribution affect the types and levels of demand.
2. Changes in world trade patterns. As the U.S. shifts from an industrial to a service economy, infrastructure needs will change.
3. Changes in technology. Advances in technology can improve services and construction techniques, but more importantly, technological changes can affect demand, e.g., more television watching has reduced the demand for libraries.
4. Changes in resource management. The availability of energy

and water will affect the types of investment decisions made by governments, and hazardous waste management may become an area of increased government involvement.

Recognizing these changes in demand, decision makers need to set priorities and control incremental costs. Use of cost/benefit analyses as an approach to controlling demand and setting priorities is useful.

Individual components should be weighed on the basis of their relative costs and benefits When choosing among individual projects, balance the value of a project in relation to its incremental benefits.[42] For new projects, the incremental cost is the entire project; for existing projects, it is the cost of operation and maintenance. However, when calculating costs and benefits, construction and annual operating expenses are not the sole costs of a project. Preventive maintenance and repair costs over the expected life of a project must also be factored in when funding a project. A survey by the National League of Cities shows only 43 percent of cities consider these costs. New York state is considering requiring that appropriations for state-funded infrastructure projects include costs for maintenance and repair over the lifespan of the projects to assure that state officials are aware of the full cost implications of new construction commitments. Vaughn and the U.S. General Accounting Office both note that cities with better infrastructure conditions use this approach.[43]

Beneficiaries of projects should bear the costs The users of a facility should bear the cost of the services provided.[44] This approach is important in limiting the demand for a project, because the investment costs are driven by the degree of usage, not by a set of engineering standards. For social reasons, a deliberate subsidy to certain classes of users may be desirable, but this should be a conscious decision on the part of policy makers and not hidden in overall cost figures.

An important corollary of the full cost recovery principle is: the share of costs paid by each user should be in proportion to the cost that user imposes. By controlling "cross-subsidies" among classes of users (e.g., subsidizing industrial wastewater costs with higher household rates), the marginal investment costs are minimized and equity among users is increased.

Financing mechanisms should be chosen in the context of each component of infrastructure Changes in infrastructure decision-making methods necessarily imply increased state and local roles. This, in turn, implies greater responsibility for financing projects at those levels and implies changes in the mechanisms of financing.

Numerous articles have been written on state and local financing alternatives. Vaughn has identified some, including:

1. Greater use of user fees
2. Dedicated revenue sources
3. Federal loans and loan guarantees
4. State bond guarantees for local debt financing
5. Creative instruments to improve access to credit markets
6. Federal, state, and regional infrastructure or development banks
7. Independent authorities, commissions, or special districts
8. Tax incentives, such as safe-harbor leasing, which would increase private sector involvement in public works financing.[45]

Is increased state-local funding possible?

The foregoing principles suggest a greater state and local responsibility for financing infrastructure. The question many observers raise in this time of increasing state and local fiscal austerity is: can states and localities afford to do it? While current financial problems may exist, capital financing based on long-term borrowing must be viewed over a longer span of time. The decline in the state-local role in infrastructure financing in recent years has contributed to a long-term decrease in state-local debt burdens. In 1971, 21 percent of own-source revenues were dedicated to debt and interest payments; in 1981 only 12 percent of own-source revenues were used for this purpose. If they historically bore a heavier burden, could they not do so in the future?

Also, one of the reasons behind the reduced state-local role, the inability to gain voter approval for new bond issues, has ameliorated over the past few years. States and localities are finding a greater approval rate. In addition, they are relying less on general obligation bonds, which require voter approval, and are relying more on revenue bonds, which do not. Therefore, states and localities seem to have the capacity to undertake a greater fiscal responsibility for their own infrastructure financing under a set of principles such as those just put forth.

Conclusion

By a variety of measures the value of the stock of state and local public infrastructure is stagnant and annual investment in new infrastructure is declining. Many analysts contend that a concerted effort to increase investment is needed to reverse these trends. However, they have often confined their analyses to changes in the supply of investment dollars without examining changes in demand.

When details of the decline in the value of capital stock are examined, we see that changing investment patterns over the past several decades stem from changes in the demand for certain forms of infrastructure. As a result, restoration of historical growth trends for infrastructure may be inappropriate to future needs. Also, the needs established via various standards may also be inappropriate. This implies that current assessments of infrastructure investment needs may be overstated.

Even so, changes in investment incentives in recent years suggest a need to reevaluate strategies by which infrastructure investment decisions are made. Changes in the financing of infrastructure have contributed to obscuring the level of government accountable or responsible for infrastructure. An investment strategy that requires a definition of responsibility, focused at the state and local level, with incentives for reduced demand, will provide a more efficient means of meeting infrastructure needs based on demonstrated demand for a project than a standards-based, federally financed approach.

1. Roger J. Vaughn, *Rebuilding America: Financing Public Works in the 1980s*, vol. 2 (Washington, D.C.: Council of State Planning Agencies, 1983), p. 4.

2. Stuart Holland, *The State as Entrepreneur* (London: Weidenfeld and Nicolson, 1972), pp. 214–216; as cited in "Emerging Issues in Financing Basic Infrastructure," unpublished paper by Michael Pagano and Richard Moore, 1981, pp. 3–4.

3. See, for instance, N. Dossani and W. Steger, "Trends in U.S. Public Works Investment: Report on a New Study," *National Tax Journal* 33:2 (June 1980), pp. 124, 139.

4. CONSAD, *A Study of Public Works Investment in the United States* (Washington, D.C.: U.S. Department of Commerce, April 1980), p. I.59; and U.S. Department of Commerce, Bureau of Economic Analysis, *Fixed Reproducible Tangible Wealth in the United States, 1925–79* (Washington, D.C.: Government Printing Office, March 1982), p. T-25.

5. Much of the data used in this analysis are historical series based upon estimates prepared by BEA. Primary data are based on U.S. Census

Bureau surveys of new construction put in place. Data are national aggregates; regional data are not available due to the size of the samples used. Data tables supporting trends cited in the text are available from the author upon request.

6. Congressional Budget Office, *Public Works Investment: Policy Options for the 1980s* (Washington, D.C.: Government Printing Office, April 1983), p. 6.

7. Pat Choate and Susan Walters, *America in Ruins: Beyond the Public Works Porkbarrel* (Washington, D.C.: Council of State Planning Agencies, 1981), pp. 15–17.

8. Both the National League of Cities in a recent survey and the ACIR dispute the assessment that a "crisis" exists. They believe the problem is manageable but do acknowledge the need for a new strategy. See: ACIR, "Financing Public Physical Infrastructure" (unpublished, November 1983), p. 39; and NLC/USCM, "Capital Budgeting and Infrastructure in American Cities: An Initial Assessment" (Washington, D.C.: National League of Cities, April 1983), p. vii.

9. Larry Hush, "Budgeting for Capital Infrastructure: Which Level of Gov-

ernment?" unpublished OMB paper, December 1982, pp. 1, 7.

10. U.S. Advisory Commission on Intergovernmental Relations, *The Federal Role in the Federal System: The Dynamics of Growth. A Crisis of Confidence and Competence* (Washington, D.C.: Government Printing Office, July 1980).

11. The displacement effect of $2.40 cited by Hush is greater than a dollar-for-dollar substitution. One explanation is that, in fact, a dollar-for-dollar substitution is occurring but its existence is spread over a much longer period than that examined by Hush. The volume of federal aid would not, therefore, decrease state and local investment by the magnitude Hush seems to suggest. The displacement effect is created by the expectation that federal aid will pay for projects. Everyone stops investing and gets in line to wait their turn for the federal aid.

12. Ron Forbes, et al., "An Analysis of Tax-Exempt Mortgage Revenue Bonds," Municipal Finance Study Group, State University of New York at Albany (unpublished paper, May 1979), appendix III.

13. U.S. General Accounting Office, "Trends and Changes in the Municipal Bond Market As They Relate to the Financing of State and Local Public Infrastructure," PAD-83-46, September 12, 1983.

14. George Peterson, "Financing the Nation's Infrastructure Requirements" (paper prepared for a conference sponsored by the National Academy of Sciences and National Academy of Engineering, February 1983), p. 16.

15. Choate and Walters, p. 30.

16. Rice Odell, "Can We Afford to Maintain Our Urban Infrastructure?" *Urban Land* 41:1 (January 1982), p. 5; and Claudia Copeland, "Infrastructure: Building and Rebuilding America's Capital Plant" (Washington, D.C.: Congressional Research Service, January 1983), p. 4.

17. CONSAD, p. I-44. However, as Hush points out, even when education

trends are backed out, trends are still downward.

18. U.S. Census Bureau data show that there are significant increases in the number of special districts (which rely on user fees), that an increased share of local revenues is derived from user fees, and that there is an increase in the use of revenue bonds to finance infrastructure. See *Government Finance, Series No. 5* (Washington, D.C.: Government Printing Office, various years).

19. CONSAD, vol. 2, "The History of Public Works," appendix II.

20. See, for instance, Jeanne McDermott, "Bridges: Back to Private Enterprise?" *Technology* (January/February 1982), pp. 16-26.

21. CONSAD, p. I.218. This study estimates that even if private sector investments which were public sector in nature (e.g., hospitals) were combined with similar public sector investments, the trends up through the mid-1970s still would be downward.

22. Quoted in Odell, p. 8.

23. Congressional Budget Office (CBO), p. 1.

24. See, for instance, the *Washington Post* series on decaying transportation infrastructure, November 21-24, 1982.

25. CBO, pp. 7-8.

26. Ibid., p. 104.

27. Choate and Walters, pp. 15-17.

28. George Peterson and Mary Miller, "Financing Urban Infrastructure: Policy Options" (Washington, D.C.: Urban Institute, March 1982), pp. 61-62.

29. CBO, p. 1.

30. "Rebuilding America's Infrastructure," *The Morgan Guaranty Survey* (July 1982), pp. 11-15.

31. Peterson and Miller, p. 36.

32. Testimony of the Associated General Contractors of America before the Subcommittee on Economic Development, U.S. House Public Works and Transportation Committee, September 15, 1982, p. 5.

33. CBO, p. 9; and Associated General

Contractors of America, "Infrastructure," *Constructor* (May 1983), pp. 33–64.

34. U.S. Department of Commerce, *1983 U.S. Industrial Outlook* (Washington, D.C.: Government Printing Office, January 1983), p. 1–14.
35. Peterson and Miller, p. 2. The Urban Institute has conducted a number of studies examining current infrastructure conditions and needs standards. In a sample of 62 jurisdictions, it encountered myriad technical problems in assessing conditions and found little comparability among these assessments. It concluded that, while the information collected could be of value to local jurisdictions, it could not be used to develop national standards. See also: George Peterson, testimony before the Subcommittee on Economic Development, U.S. House Public Works and Transportation Committee, September 15, 1982, pp. 11, 16.
36. Vaughn, pp. 34–36.
37. ACIR, *The Federal Role in the Federal System: The Dynamics of Growth: An Agenda for Restoring Confidence and Competence*, p. 144; and the National Conference on State Legislatures, *How States Can Assist Local Governments with Debt Financing for Infrastructure*, Legislative Finance Paper no. 9 (Denver, CO: NCSL, October 1982).
38. Congressional Budget Office, *The Federal Government in a Federal System: Current Intergovernmental Programs and Options for Change* (Washington, D.C.: Government Printing Office, August 1983), pp. 30–31.
39. Suzanne Schneider, "Considering Public Works Investment: Framework and Overview" (unpublished, December 1982).
40. Ibid., p. 15.
41. Vaughn, pp. 34–35.
42. Schneider, p. 13.
43. Roger Vaughn and Robert Pollard, *Rebuilding America: Planning and Managing Public Works in the 1980s*, vol. 1 (draft, June 1983), pp. 84–86; and U.S. General Accounting Office, "Effective Planning and Budgeting Practices Can Help Arrest the Nation's Deteriorating Public Infrastructure," PAD-83-2, November 18, 1982, pp. 53–54.
44. Rochelle Stanfield, "The Users May Have to Foot the Bill to Patch Crumbling Public Facilities," *National Journal* (November 27, 1982), p. 2016.
45. Vaughn, vol. 1, beginning on p. 171; and CONSAD, beginning on p. I-134.

Synchronized Policy Planning and Budgeting

Arlyne S. Bernhard and M. Leanne Lachman

The system developed by the City of Milwaukee, Wisconsin, for allocating Community Development Block Grant (CDBG) funds syn-
chronizes multiyear budgeting and comprehensive planning. The
system has been in place six years and is meeting the needs of
elected officials, city department heads, community representatives
and recipients of CDBG funding. As a result, community development programs are mutually reinforcing and have had a significant
impact on the city's problems.[1] Cooperation, not confrontation, exists among funding recipients, thereby making it possible to get the
maximum effect from dollars expended.

The system described in this article deals with CDBG funds
used collaboratively with other federal, state and local funds where
CDBG monies are primarily used to fund well-documented needs
that cannot be met by other sources. The system would be just as
applicable to tie together other multifund resources to respond to
well-defined needs. The system is particularly well-suited to block
grant funding where policymakers must choose between competing
needs and solutions. Because of this broad applicability, we have
used Milwaukee's experience to draw general conclusions about the
crucial components of a synchronized policy planning and budgeting
process.

First, a brief description of Milwaukee's process as it evolved.
In the mid-1970s, the Department of City Development (the agency
responsible for planning, public housing, urban renewal and physical and economic planning) undertook a new comprehensive planning effort. This resulted in a redefinition of the comprehensive
plan and Common Council approval of the first product of the plan,

Reprinted with permission from the September 1984 issue of *Governmental Finance*.

a citywide strategy that focused on preservation of the city's economic base and residential neighborhoods.

Then, in 1978, the Funding Allocation Guide was developed to assure that CDBG monies were spent in support of the city's preservation plan. The Funding Allocation Guide defines geographic areas of the city in which the funds are to be spent, the program categories and the proportion of the total grant to be spent in each program category.

The guide operates on a three-year cycle because 1978 CDBG regulations required three-year planning; but, more importantly, because the city's needs were so vast that single-year efforts would not assure enough program mass to accomplish the desired results. The guide is maintained by a task force consisting of two city council members, the relevant city department heads and two community representatives. It is adopted by the Common Council.

Each year applicants for funds are told the program category under which their projects fall, and they compete for funding. The Common Council has the final say in selecting projects but works within the categorical allocations of the guide.

Because sources and amounts of funds change, as do the actors in the implementation process and the needs of individual geographic areas, it is essential to have a rational system of allocating funds. Otherwise, cities end up with a wide range of projects serving special interests; some needs are met while others are neglected; programs often work at cross-purposes; staff time is wasted as proposals are prepared for $15 million of competing projects when only $3 million are available; and departments battle to support growing empires without regard for the city's current needs. When resources are scarce, a much more cost-effective, noncompetitive way to streamline the allocation of funds is needed, and this is where Milwaukee's comprehensive plan and Funding Allocation Guide have proven so effective.

In fact, by using this dual approach, Milwaukee did not just stay afloat through changes in federal policy, aldermen, departmental officials and community perceptions; the city saw a dramatic improvement in the central city's homes and neighborhoods and created a new spirit of cooperation between the city and community groups.

Identifying problems and recognizing opportunities

Milwaukee's comprehensive plan is a series of documents with goals, policies and objectives and, where applicable, land use maps to guide planning, programming and budgeting decisions. The plan will never be complete because it must be revised as the city changes and new challenges and opportunities emerge. Once consensus is reached on goals and policies, though, seminars and briefings are

> *Exhibit 1. The comprehensive plan.*
>
> **Level I**
> Citywide strategy
>
> **Level II**
> Citywide goals and policies
>
> **Level III**
> Subarea goals and policies
>
> **Level IV**
> Neighborhood goals and policies

held with operating departments so that as many current programming and budgeting decisions as possible serve to reinforce each other. Written documents have a lower priority because city officials grasp policies and guiding principles much better when they can talk them through, asking questions and discussing tangible examples. Exhibit 1 shows the four levels of the comprehensive plan. Each succeeding level gives increasingly specific guidance and is consistent with the assumptions of preceding levels.

As support for these policy planning levels, Milwaukee developed an extensive information base and series of analyses[2] to explain the behavior of generic functions within the city. Because more than half the city's land is devoted to residential uses, the housing function assumed top priority in the planning process.

As was happening in other older cities in the early 1970s, Milwaukee was losing population and gaining households. Unlike other similar cities, though, Milwaukee contained substantial undeveloped and essentially suburban land from earlier annexations. Also, it had experienced neither widespread abandonment of standard houses nor extensive neighborhood decay. Milwaukee did not want development of the vacant land to be at the expense of the older neighborhoods: The activities under the city's jurisdiction should reinforce existing neighborhoods and support property values throughout the city.

At this point, the Department of City Development (DCD) presented to the Common Council the proposed Preservation Policy for the City of Milwaukee. Because the need to maintain the existing building stock was explicitly given priority over new construction, a consensus was reached among elected officials, neighborhood organizations and city staff. The principles of the Preservation Policy shown in Exhibit 2 became the guiding forces behind Milwaukee's community development decisions from 1978 on.

DCD's analysis and data base became the monitoring system that provided an ongoing context for targeting residential strate-

> *Exhibit 2. The six principles of Milwaukee's preservation policy.*
>
> Maintain present housing, jobs, neighborhoods, services and tax base while taking advantage of realistic development opportunities.
>
> • Create new jobs and retain existing ones.
> • Support all neighborhoods according to need.
> • Limit new residential construction and guide its location.
> • Improve living conditions in the central city.
> • Cooperate with neighborhood organizations.
> • Create stable, economically integrated neighborhoods.

gies and developing community and official support for those strategies. Relative measures were designed to show how residential areas differed, where various types of households were located, the diversity of housing conditions and the financial needs of households in different neighborhoods. The city's residential areas were disaggregated into subareas with similar characteristics. The geographic clustering of residential areas and different types of households gave planners important clues as to problems and opportunities and made it possible for decision makers to understand the entire housing system as well as individual neighborhoods.

The analyses were considered "developed" when those most familiar with the neighborhoods said that DCD's map coincided with their experiences. Once residents and elected officials felt that their neighborhoods were accurately portrayed, they trusted descriptions of areas with which they were less familiar. Most important, they could see the interrelationships within the housing market and came to understand that the fate of their neighborhoods rested, in part, with actions occurring elsewhere in the city.

The ability to synchronize the work on the comprehensive plan with the Funding Allocation Guide was largely due to three traits of comprehensive planning in Milwaukee.

1. The comprehensive plan begins at the citywide level, not in the neighborhoods. Conflicts between neighborhoods are minimized when council members and residents understand the relationship of their areas to the whole of the city. Further, starting citywide means that the budget system can be tied to implementation as soon as the citywide strategy is adopted.
2. Indicators and trend analyses must be tailored specifically to each city. Growing Sun Belt and shrinking Midwest cities cannot look at the same set of indicators if unique problems and opportunities are to emerge. Regularly repeated analyses offer a way of reviewing updated local conditions and evaluating programs already underway. Properly designed moni-

toring permits rapid identification of unforeseen problems and assures that responses are not made in a vacuum. These data were invaluable in determining Milwaukee's community development funding needs.

3. Consultants provide the national expertise and long-range perspectives that provide a context for a city's decision-making. Once Milwaukee defined its problems (the longest and most expensive part of the process), it needed consultants with national experience to help define opportunities and recommend programs. Some distance from day-to-day planning is essential to comprehensive planning. Even the senior staff most knowledgeable about the larger issues tend to forget them in the face of daily pressures.

Bringing together policy, programs and budgets

Shortly after the Common Council adopted the Preservation Policy, the U.S. Department of Housing and Urban Development required a three-year plan for the CDBG program. This requirement provided Milwaukee with an excellent opportunity to tie the comprehensive plan to a major implementation resource, using the Funding Allocation Guide as the vehicle.

The funding guide serves two major purposes: (1) to assure that CDBG regulations are met through programs and projects that are consonant with the city's defined preservation needs; and (2) to see that a critical mass of programs is focused on neighborhoods in a coordinated way so that the intended benefits are realized. The Funding Allocation Guide sets three-year program and budget goals, but the task force meets annually to evaluate the program's progress.

The multiyear plan provides program flexibility. The guide does not specify what projects should be submitted in each of the program categories. City departments and noncity agencies still compete and have freedom for innovation. Some schedule their projects in equal increments while others plan more uneven work loads, especially in the early years of a new project. The guide's three-year time horizon enabled DCD, for example, to establish intensive treatment areas where a year of planning and organization could be followed by a year or so of acquisition and rehabilitation.

The housing monitoring system provides data that permit individual projects to be redesigned to increase effectiveness. For example, in the early years of the first guide, a 20-year standard for housing rehabilitation was common. But the high cost and the vast need for small repairs to many houses led to the development of a five-year standard, which was less ambitious for an individual residence but more effective for the neighborhood. Cheap, direct repair services were expanded so that more units could be worked on annually.

Analysis of the guide after the first three years showed that program categories actually were funded at the levels suggested by the guide and that the performance goals were met. Monitoring confirmed positive changes in Milwaukee's neighborhoods. Rapid deterioration in the poorest areas was stopped, and physical appearance was much improved; and stronger parts of the central city no longer needed intensive special programming.

There are three major program categories in the guide: planning and management, social services and physical development programs. The guide clearly favors physical development programs, putting dollar limits on the other two categories.

The task force's needs analysis showed substantial physical housing problems, and neighborhood service groups were enlisted to join the city in providing assistance. Major changes to the physical plant are done by the city, but neighborhood groups offer a wide range of direct services to homes and families. (In Milwaukee, social services are primarily the responsibility of other units of government and private agencies.)

When the size of the total grants began to diminish, in later years, city officials and community leaders determined that housing rehabilitation needs were so pervasive that nonrehabilitation requests had to be scaled back so that a meaningful mass of housing programs could still be funded. Capital improvements, a major thrust of pre-task-force CDBG programming, became secondary to housing programs.

DCD staff developed a list of broad program categories to meet the physical needs of the neighborhoods and analyzed delivery capability for the CDBG area. As shown in Exhibit 3, the task force ranked the program categories high, medium and low, depending on their relative importance in meeting the Preservation Policy, availability of non-CDBG funds and the ability to perform the tasks.

In the first guide, there were sufficient funds for all categories ranked high and a portion of those ranked medium. The second guide covered a period of declining funds, so reductions were made in each category, following a percentage formula. All program categories included in the final guide have timetables, measurable objectives and category budgets.

Almost all the physical program categories were funded by a percentage fair share formula. Percentages were derived during the needs analysis and ranking steps. Each category is assigned the percentage of the expected grant to assure the level of funding needed. The percentage formula was necessary so that each physical development subcategory could be adjusted automatically when dollar amounts of the grant fluctuated.

Critical to the successful preparation of the guide was the task force's ability to reach consensus on the priority rankings for the

Exhibit 3. Milwaukee's task force rankings for physical development
program categories.

Subcategories	Task force ranking
1. Code enforcement	High
2. Animal/rodent control	High
3. Vacant land maintenance	High
4. Housing rehabilitation	High
5. Housing production	High
6. Land acquisition	High
7. Commercial and economic development	High
8. Capital improvements	
Sidewalks	High
Street lighting improvements	High
Playground construction	High
Public facilities and/or paving	Medium
Sewers	Low
Bridges	Low
9. Public housing modernization	Low

physical program categories and the emphasis on physical programs over planning/management and social services. Agreement
was reached efficiently because task force members took the time to
familiarize themselves with the economic and demographic conditions of the city before they developed an implementation strategy.
Further, the task force encouraged frank discussion of participants'
"mental maps" about what Milwaukee could or should become.

Milwaukee officials used four ground rules for communication
in the budgeting and planning process:

1. Solutions cannot be discussed until problems and opportuni-
    ties are understood. This means breaking the natural ten-
    dency of a task force to move quickly toward solutions. By
    restricting early meetings to descriptions of the conditions in
    the city, consensus was forged quickly. Then, the "what to do"
    sessions also moved ahead efficiently because all the parties
    —citizens, elected officials and city staff—could see that the
    alternatives were limited. They also had the Preservation
    Policy adopted by the council so that there was a framework
    for undertaking consistent and mutually reinforcing imple-
    mentation programs.

2. All people involved in implementation should be represented
    in the planning process. Milwaukee's Funding Allocation
    Guide task force consists of the heads of affected city depart-
    ments, the president of the Common Council, the chairman of

the council committee charged with reviewing the CDBG program, the mayor's office and two citizens. Once adopted, after extensive hearings, the funding guide has been followed scrupulously by the Common Council.

3.   Participants must face up to their own impressions of what the city can be. After agreement is reached on problems, the suggestions of both opportunities and action alternatives will vary substantially if participants have different ideas about the city's future. It is essential that these differences be discussed in a supportive environment, which may include private meetings as well as general sessions. Actually, if a task force follows the approach described above, differences about action choices usually are minimized.

4.   Leadership is essential to resolve apparent impasses. A variety of techniques can be used here. Behind-the-scenes meetings often are critical in accomplishing trade-offs. Also, consultants or outside, unbiased experts can be useful in presenting information on current conditions and available alternative actions as well as in facilitating the entire process.

Conclusions

The Milwaukee experience presents a strong case for synchronized comprehensive planning and budgeting. At maximum, the model could be used to integrate all city budgets. In summary, here are the merits of this approach:

1.   Individual departments and community groups do a better job of focusing their work when an explicit plan is understood and when results are periodically evaluated.

2.   A coordinated strategy results in: (1) targeting of programs to the areas most in need; (2) concentration of mutually reinforcing programs; and (3) allocation of sufficient resources to have the desired effect.

3.   Participants become less defensive about protecting their turfs. In Milwaukee, for example, the commissioner of public works supported cuts in his department's activities in order to increase housing rehabilitation. Aldermen and citizens also were willing to forgo projects in their own neighborhoods to allow intensive focus on more distressed areas.

4.   The city sees where outside dollars must be generated, and new federal, state or local programs can easily be integrated into a well-defined strategy. At the same time, when regulations for a federal or state program are not in the city's best interest, negotiation can be based on evidence rather than perceptions.

5. Because the actors in the process inevitably change, a city-wide strategy has to be redescribed and reaffirmed periodically. This can be a component of a regular evaluation and update.

The Funding Allocation Guide is so popular with Milwaukee decision makers that it is now the catalyst for the entire planning process. No one wants to return to the days of dealing with uncoordinated and unrealistic proposals that do not relate to a city strategy.

1. Arlyne S. Bernhard and M. Leanne Lachman, "Milwaukee: Neighborhood Preservation in Action," *Urban Land*, vol. 42, no. 12 (December 1983), pp. 16-19.
2. For a discussion of a monitoring system, see: Arlyne S. Bernhard, Randolf A. Gschwind and William G. Huxhold, "Developing Policy Management Information Systems," URISA, August 1983; and Donald S. Cannon, M. Leanne Lachman and Arlyne S. Bernhard, "Identifying Neighborhoods for Preservation and Renewal," *Growth and Change*, vol. 8, no. 1, pp. 35-38; and Department of City Development, *Relative Residential Status in Milwaukee in 1975 and 1980*, May 1983.

PART 4

Fiscal
Forecasting

Organizing and Implementing a Forecasting Function

Steven C. Wheelwright and Spyros Makridakis

Editor's note: Although written from the point of view of a private-sector organization, this article contains sound advice for local governments.

The first section of this article examines some of the elements of an ongoing forecasting procedure to identify the skills and resources that are required within the organization to carry out that function successfully. The next section deals with the forecasting function and its sponsorship within the organization. It includes an analysis not only of the staff support needed for forecasting but also the role in it of other parts of the organization. The third section deals with the behavioral aspect of forecasting. Since people are involved in the forecasting function, these behavioral aspects are important considerations. This section focuses on some of the more important considerations in this area that are essential to the successful implementation of forecasting systems. The final section examines some of the characteristics of successful forecasting applications and how an organization might apply itself to getting started.

The emphasis here is on those aspects of the forecasting function that are most important to the manager. Clearly there are details associated with establishing a staff organization to support forecasting that must be known by the individual who will be in charge of that group. This article, however, does not deal at that level of detail but rather aims at covering the main points that are important to the manager (user) of that forecasting support group.

Elements of an ongoing forecasting procedure

In any specific forecasting application six basic steps or elements will generally be followed. These six steps are important considerations in establishing the forecasting function because support must be made available for each of them. If any of these steps is omitted or not properly supported, the results of forecasting will not be completely satisfactory. To see just what skills and resources are required for the forecasting function we shall examine each of these six steps in turn.

1. Identification of management requirements for a forecast
The starting point on any new forecasting application is an identification of management's requirements. Because of the nature of forecasting and the supportive role it plays in decision making, the forecasting staff group will frequently identify what they think is a need and then on asking management about it will naturally receive a positive reply; that is, since supplying a manager with a forecast does not require any explicit change in his decision making, he can always say he would like more information, whether or not that information is directly relevant to his problem. Following such a procedure in the development of new forecasting applications can be detrimental to the forecasting function in the long run. When the forecasting staff group identifies the potential needs, it is likely that the number of forecasts being supplied to management will increase rapidly, yet the effect on management's decision making will be only minimal.

What is needed at this stage is a procedure that will require the manager's participation in determining what forecasts would be most useful in his specific situation. Although it will clearly be harder to involve a busy manager in this identification process, those firms that have done so have found it much more profitable in the long run. One approach that has been used successfully has been to have the staff group initiate interest in forecasting by holding discussion sessions with small groups of managers. The purpose of these sessions is to introduce managers to some of the possibilities that exist in the application of forecasting. This is then followed with a procedure in which managers themselves will identify what they think may be appropriate situations for forecasting. A staff person can then meet on a one-to-one basis with the manager to discuss the possible applications and to identify the one or two that look most promising.

2. Competent support staff In any medium-to-large organization it is attractive to have a specific staff group of one or more people to help in the development and application of forecasting.

The main tasks of this group are to support each of the steps of forecasting as a catalyst and to be responsible for the actual data collection and the application of specific techniques in a given situation. It is imperative that its members be competent in their understanding of the available forecasting methods and that they also be competent in understanding management problems. In most cases their training will have been on the technical side, but it is still of the utmost importance that they be able to discuss with the manager his problems and situations in order to fit the most appropriate forecasting technique to that application.

The problems attendant on the development of such a staff group are similar to those that accompany the development of an operations research group or some other technical group designed to support management efforts. In general companies have found that it is better to trade technical expertise for an understanding of the management task in setting up these groups; that is, one would much rather have a person who is of average competence in the various techniques of forecasting and very good at discussing these techniques and their appropriateness for different situations with management. It is important that management understand that this staff group has been established to support them in their work and that they can call on them when necessary. Whenever additional stumbling blocks appear in getting support from this group, managers will find other ways of acquiring the information they need (or go without it). Thus the organization must supply the staff support and make it available directly to those managers who can potentially apply forecasting.

3. Data collection One characteristic of successful forecasting is that the manager who becomes involved in the development of a new application wants to see results. Whenever it takes several months or even years to obtain these results, the manager will tend to lose interest. In the data collection area this means that support must be available, either in the form of a data base or in terms of a willingness to acquire published sources of data so that new applications of forecasting can provide forecasts soon after they are identified. Although there are exceptions when a manager will be willing to wait a considerable length of time to initiate a new forecasting procedure, in general it is best when first applying forecasting with a given manager to select an application for which data can be collected rapidly.

The actual collection of data will generally be under the direction of the forecasting staff group and may be performed by them or by someone in the accounting group. The actual person doing the collecting of the data will be determined by its type and source. Clearly, if the data is related to the accounting system, it would be best to get the accounting people to collect it. If, however, it comes from a single outside source not currently being used, it is generally more efficient to have the forecasting staff collect that data themselves.

Once the procedure has been established for the actual collection of the data, it must be put into form for applying the forecasting method. This will generally involve getting the data into the computer system or a local service bureau so that a computerized version of the forecasting method can be applied. The design of this data collection and formatting operation is one of the key technical functions of the forecasting staff.

4. Applying the forecasting method to the data Once the data has been collected, the forecasting staff can then apply the appropriate method of forecasting to that data. Again, this is a technical problem and is best handled by the staff. It is important, however, that the manager understand the underlying features of the method that is being applied and recognize the strengths and weaknesses of that forecasting procedure.

At this stage it is generally essential that the organization supply the necessary computer support needed to prepare these forecasts efficiently. This support will generally include not only computer time but also some initial time of a programmer to fit the forecasting method to the available data. Sometimes a member of the forecasting staff will be capable of doing the programming himself. In larger organizations the importance of having a forecasting staff that can effectively communicate with management makes it more attractive to have such people spend a large portion of their time with the manager and his problems and use specialists in the task of programming.

5. Communicating the forecast to the manager In order for a forecast to be of maximum usefulness it must be given to the manager when he needs it and in the form that will fit his decision-making situation. This requires that the forecasting staff be fully aware of the time frame within which the manager will operate and have sufficient rapport with him that he will call them if that time frame changes. In terms of the format in which the forecast is presented it is always useful not only to supply the manager with the single forecast but also with some of the assumptions inherent in the data and the method used. Thus, if there were some special problem in getting the data for this forecast and if the staff had some doubts about the accuracy of that data, the manager should be made aware of it. One thing that should clearly be avoided is overloading the manager with information. It is not generally necessary to give him a complete listing of all of the data used in preparing the forecast but rather to highlight those factors of which he should be aware.

6. Feedback and comparison of actual results to forecast results To measure the effectiveness of a forecasting application it is necessary to compare the actual results with those that were forecast. This can generally be done by setting up a periodic review procedure. For these reviews the forecasting staff must analyze the errors in the forecast and any trends that may be apparent in the errors. It should be a staff responsibility to perform this initial analysis and then to sit down with the manager and reassess the usefulness of the forecast and the opportunities for improving it for that situation. It may also be useful to record the manager's subjective modifications to the staff forecast, assess the accuracy of these modifications and then feedback this information to improve the modification process in the future.

A good checklist for establishing a forecasting function or appraising an existing function is to consider the six steps outlined above and the level of support available in each one. It is easy for an ongoing procedure to treat one or more of these steps lightly and thus reduce the effectiveness of that forecasting procedure.

Forecasting organization and sponsorship

A good starting point in the development of a forecasting function is to analyze the organization's preparedness for such a function. Clearly some are in a much better position to initiate a formal forecasting operation than are others. The three factors that determine preparedness are top management's attitude, middle management's attitude, and the competence of the forecasting staff. If all three of these factors are considerably above average, the success of forecasting is much more likely. Even if these three factors are only average, there is still a good chance that forecasting can be applied successfully. If, however, any one of these factors is below average, the organization is best advised not to go ahead with a formalized forecasting setup.

In determining just where the organization stands on these three factors it is necessary to perform an actual analysis. In determining the attitude of middle management and top management toward forecasting, it is not enough just to ask them what their views are. Forecasting is like many other fads and everyone feels that they should be interested in it. However, in performing an analysis on one's own organization, it is necessary to ask specific managers why they think it would be useful and just what it would do for them. This kind of questioning frequently points up that everyone thinks it is a good idea but that for one reason or another it would not be appropriate in their own situations. When one management group is not sold on the usefulness of forecasting, an educational phase can often be undertaken to help management understand the value of planning and controlling operations and the usefulness of forecasts in this function.

When the organization identifies a problem of staff incompetency, the only solution is to bring in new blood or to wait the several months to a couple of years necessary to train the existing staff. Most firms have found that initiating a forecasting function in parallel with the training of a staff is not effective. It is much more appropriate to develop competence at the staff level before undertaking forecasting to aid management.

After the fact, managers are always amazed at the extraordinary problems that can develop in getting a forecasting procedure initiated and working effectively. Overcoming some of them is often more than a matter of simply reorganizing the project. For one thing personalities can often be the cause and cannot be changed overnight. Simply redrawing the organization chart will not solve most underlying problems. However, a number of them seem to occur regularly in forecasting and an examination of the experience of several companies in these areas can help those establishing a forecasting procedure to avoid them. They include the following:

1. People make mistakes in recording data and thus the decision maker is understandably reluctant to base decisions on that data.
2. Those whose job it is to check a forecast may only rubber stamp it and simply pass it on without adequately verifying its reliability.
3. The decision maker may find that the forecasting data never seems to be available in time for his decisions.
4. The decision maker may not be committed to the forecast and to its use because he does not understand it.
5. Many of the individuals whose contribution is required to make forecasting successful do not feel any personal need for making those changes in their own procedures that are necessary to complete the forecasting system.
6. On occasion the wrong forecasting approach may have been adopted and thus the experts in the firm are reluctant to push for its implementation.

There are four general areas in which careful planning and support can be done to help eliminate such problems. These areas involve the allocation of responsibility. They determine who will make decisions, specify who is to pay for forecasting applications, and determine who will do the work. Each of these areas is discussed in turn.

Who is responsible? A major mistake that companies often make in establishing a forecasting function is never to define clearly the responsibility and leadership for it. Oftentimes executives just hope that this responsibility will find its own home in due time. This approach, however, can often cause tremendous misunderstanding and thus give a bad orientation toward forecasting right from the start.

The responsibility for developing forecasting applications and a forecasting function must be given to a member of the management team. This will generally involve the individual either in charge of accounting and control or of other systems activities. There is no set rule about the area that is most appropriate in general. Rather an organization is well advised to examine its own experience in terms of how other parts have been patterned; for example, if it has done well with projects in which a staff individual has been put in charge, then this same organization will probably work well in the forecasting area. If, however, the organization as a general rule puts such staff responsibility under an operating manager, then it should seek to be consistent in this area as well. The key is to make sure that one person is responsible for the success of the function and that he has the authority to take the actions necessary to guarantee success.

Who makes decisions? There are two kinds of decisions to be made in connection with the forecasting function. One, which was mentioned in the preceding paragraph, involves guiding the entire function in the organization. In this case a single individual must be given the authority to make the guiding decisions.

The other type of decision involves specific projects and applications of forecasting. The difficulty here is to decide which decisions will be under the control of the forecasting staff and which under the control of the manager, or user, of that particular forecast. One consideration is who will be available when they need to be made. Many of the smaller technical decisions clearly should fall under the direction of the forecasting staff. Major technical decisions, however, should at least be reviewed by the manager who will use the forecast. Thus it is not at all inappropriate to involve the manager in the choice of a forecasting method.

Some of the areas in which it is clearly the manager's responsibility to make decisions include determining the applications for which forecasts are to be prepared and the frequency with which they are needed. As a general rule, companies have found that the best division of this decision-making responsibility is to have the forecasting staff act as a catalyst in getting the decisions made, and to recommend what they think is best, but to let the user of the forecast have the final word on any major decision.

Even in ongoing situations, it is important that the decision-making responsibilities be agreed on by both the staff and the operating people. This can be viewed largely as an educational task of informing those involved just what constitutes acceptable behavior and what seems to have worked most effectively in other situations.

Who pays for forecasting projects?   Assigning the cost of forecasting applications to specific departments and organizational units is an important aspect in the forecasting function. There will generally be some overhead cost associated with the maintenance of a forecasting staff, but the majority of the expense should be assignable to specific projects. Experience has shown that it is important to allocate these costs whenever possible to the organizational unit making use of a forecast. The main advantage of doing this is that the operating manager will then be much more likely to evaluate the benefits of the forecast in contrast to its cost than he would otherwise. When an organizational unit does not have to pay for having a forecast prepared, it will usually justify any forecast as having value, even if it is only marginal.

As a part of the cost allocation process, the initial analysis of a forecasting application should include the development of a budget for that application and the user's agreement to cover its cost. The forecasting staff can then be evaluated in terms of their staying within the budget and accomplishing the objectives outlined for the project, and the user of the forecast can have a firm idea of what he will be charged for.

In those situations in which a forecast is being supplied to several different organizational units, as is often done at the start of the long-range planning cycle, most companies have found that the best procedure is to assign the cost of that forecast as they would the project as a whole. Thus, if the cost of long-range planning is simply charged to general overhead, the forecasts supplied in connection with that planning project should be handled in a similar manner. On the other hand, if the costs are generally allocated to individual departments, so should the forecasting costs.

Who does the work?   Three functions are involved in any forecasting application: the forecasting staff that identifies and carries out applications of forecasting, the management user who will apply that forecast to his own situation, and the computer group that will actually apply the forecasting method to the data. To coordinate the efforts of these different people, it is essential that one person have the responsibility for seeing that the project is completed on schedule and that procedures are established for coordinating the various units. Generally the individual to be placed in charge of the project will be a member of the forecasting staff. Since he has the technical background and the interface with the management user, he is in the best position to coordinate these activities.

Perhaps the most common problem in assigning the work is scheduling the computer support time. Since the computer group is also a staff group, it is often difficult for the forecasting people to get the kind of response from the computer staff that they need to be effective. One solution to this problem is to have both staff groups reporting to the same individual. An alternative solution is simply to set up procedures that state firmly when forecasting projects will be worked on and give the time schedule that must be met by the computer group in those applications.

One approach that has been used quite effectively in forecasting is the development of a project team. Although many forecasting situations are small and really require the support of only a couple of people, in other projects in which the forecast will be used by several organizational units it is helpful to have a team whose responsibility is the success of the project. This project team can serve as a communications system for progress being made in the development of the application and will ensure that the application will meet the requirements of the users. The project team also provides a means of exposing several different people in the firm to forecasting and its usefulness.

Characteristics of successful forecasting situations

The preceding sections have outlined a number of steps that can be taken by the manager and by individuals responsible for forecasting to improve the likelihood that it will be useful in a particular situation. Also a number of more general steps and simple problem attributes are associated with the successful application of forecasting. These deal with three areas: the type of manager involved, the general level of support within the organization, and the forecasting situation itself.

As we would anticipate, the level of success in applying formalized forecasting methods is closely related to the type of manager involved in the forecasting situation. Three things that generally characterize a manager who successfully implements forecasting are, first, that he understands the situation for which the forecast is being prepared and knows what is required for successful decision making in that area. This ensures that the forecast is in a meaningful area and that he will feel comfortable about using it in that type of situation. A second characteristic is that the manager must be interested in real improvements in decision making. A manager who simply implements a forecasting procedure because his boss thought it would be a good idea will never be so successful as the manager who adopts forecasting because he really wants to improve his decision making. The third characteristic is that the manager must understand the forecasting technique and its value. Even in a large organization in which adequate staff support is available it is only when the manager takes the time to become familiar with the forecasting technique and its strengths and weaknesses that the forecast will have significant value.

The second aspect of a successful forecasting application is the environment. There are several things that an organization can do to support formalized forecasting applications. These include communicating successful applications to others in the organization, which indicates that the organization is concerned with forecasting and takes note of those who are successful in using it. Another is training managers on various forecasting techniques and the general procedures for adapting them to their own situations. Top management also needs to give support and encouragement to such applications. Finally, the organization must give the manager access to those resources that are required to utilize forecasting. These resources include historical data (and manpower to update the data), specialists in the area of formal forecasting techniques, and computer support to help in the actual preparation of the forecast. All these things can help to make the organization a more likely environment in which forecasting will be successfully used.

Finally, the situation itself is important to ensure the success of forecasting. Situations must be chosen that are helpful to the manager, that provide the opportunity for reducing uncertainty, and in which the value of improvements in decision making is substantial. Although it may be easier to use forecasting on well-established problems in which historical data is available, it is often the case that decision-making procedures in such areas are also well developed, and thus there is little room for improvement even with formal forecasting. What is needed are situations in which the opportunity for improvement exists and in which the manager involved is the kind of person who would like to improve the decision making in that area.

The Role of Multi-Year Forecasting in the Annual Budgeting Process

Roy Bahl and Larry Schroeder

The annual budget focuses on a single twelve-month period, yet spending and revenue decisions made today can have long-lasting fiscal effects. New capital projects require future spending on operations, maintenance, and debt-carrying charges; altered pension benefits carry long-term commitments; new fee structures will influence later years' revenues; and hiring, layoff, and salary schedule decisions have fiscal impacts well beyond the year in which they are made. Despite these very obvious long-term implications, surprisingly few local governments have attempted systematically to link the annual budget to a multi-year fiscal plan.

Multi-year projections of revenues and expenditures are a necessary step in overcoming the myopic attitudes often exhibited in the annual budget process. Projections do not, by themselves, constitute a multi-year fiscal plan, but they are both the first step and the major building block in preparing long-term budget plans. This article argues that local governments can prepare and effectively use revenue and expenditure forecasts in the annual budget process and reports the successful experience in a group of large cities. It begins by briefly describing the techniques which can be used to derive three- to five-year forecasts of spending and revenues. The experiences of several large cities which use such projection efforts are then reviewed to show how the results have been directly applied in preparation of the annual budget. Finally, the role of forecasts in budgetary policy making is summarized.

Reprinted with permission from the spring 1984 issue of *Public Budgeting & Finance*. The article is an outgrowth of work on revenue and expenditure forecasting under a grant from the National Science Foundation (DAR78-20256).

Multi-year forecasting techniques[1]

The most common approach to budgetary forecasting involves assuming a "business as usual" scenario. That is, one attempts to project the growth in revenues and expenditures over the next three to five years if no new policy initiatives are undertaken; i.e., no tax rate changes, no service level alterations, no real compensation increases. This approach provides an estimate of how the future budgetary position of the jurisdiction will be affected by external factors which are beyond the control of the local government (inflation, federal aid, etc.). The exercise produces less a forecast of what actually will occur then a set of baseline projections which can be used to simulate the effects of policy changes.

Several different techniques have been used to generate such projections. These might be classified as judgmental, trend, deterministic, and econometric. Cities which have implemented multi-year forecasting programs use some combination of these four approaches.

The two most straightforward approaches rely on observations of past performance. Under the judgmental approach to forecasting, an individual or several individuals (often the budget officer and staff) are consulted as to their "best guess" concerning the probable level of a particular revenue or expenditure category. That best guess becomes the forecast. For example, intergovernmental grants are often forecast using a judgmental approach. Expert judgments are sometimes the best approach to forecasting, but of course the results are only as good as the expert. In any case, this approach is much less useful for a multi-year forecast than for making revenue projections for the annual budget. Trend techniques are a bit more systematic in that they project the future from the historical movement in a revenue or expenditure series. The technique is simple and can be accurate, especially when the series that is forecast does not fluctuate with the changing economic and demographic fortunes of the community.

Deterministic approaches allow the analyst more opportunity to build policy assumptions directly into the forecast. For example, an automobile registration revenue is equivalent to an automobile registration fee times the number of autos registered; hence, a deterministic technique requires only that future values of the multiplicands be forecast. Labor expenditures in a department require that one project, separately, the amount of employment and the average compensation level. The advantage of simplicity argues for such an approach.

At the other end of the spectrum are the econometric techniques which rely upon relationships between revenues/expenditures and a set of "independent" socioeconomic variables. By assuming future values of these socioeconomic variables, the econometric technique yields a projection of the fiscal series under the assumption that the same functional relationship will hold in the future. The econometric approach is more costly in terms of data and computational and statistical expertise requirements, more difficult to explain to laymen and the city council, and probably useful only for the revenue side of the budget. On the other hand, it has many advantages. It permits an estimate of the impact of economic fluctuations on economically sensitive revenues, it enables one to simulate the fiscal impact of varying degrees of recession and inflation, and it leads to a better understanding of the underlying relationship between the local economic base and the local fiscal structure.

Expenditure forecasting and budgeting

Most local government fiscal planning systems attempt to forecast a "constant services" level of expenditures. Even though few can say what this really means, the forecasts project what it would cost to deliver a package of services comparable to that provided in a base year. The question, in other words, is "how much will it cost us to continue doing what we are doing now?" In practice, this approach involves projecting the effects of price increases, population shifts, and any planned service changes. The projection method is detailed but not particularly complicated. It amounts to little more than multiplication and addition—summing across all spending categories the product of prices of inputs times the quantities likely to be purchased in the future. Even though most cities that project expenditures use this deterministic, accounting-identity approach, there are important differences in the specific techniques employed. The simplest approach relies almost entirely on inflation to drive the forecasts, while more sophisticated models take both real inputs and price levels into account.

Expenditure forecasts are linked to the anticipated inflation in New Orleans[2] and, to a lesser extent, in the District of Columbia[3] and New York City.[4] In these cities there is a recognition that real inputs are unlikely to be permitted to expand much in the near term and that the driving force behind spending increases will be price level rises.[5]

This inflation-driven approach to expenditure forecasting has proved useful in the annual budget process. In each of the three cities mentioned, the expenditure forecasts have been computerized so that alternative inflation rates can be applied to labor and various categories of nonpersonal spending. Furthermore, each city produces an initial run-through of the expenditure forecast—including a one-year forecast—even before the formal budget process begins. In New York City this is a part of its mandated multi-year forecasting procedure, while in New Orleans and the District of Columbia the exercise is for internal policy-making use. It is on the basis of these initial projections that budgetary instructions are given, such as estimates of the total amount available to an agency in the following fiscal year. Moreover, since the process is computerized, policy makers can easily make additional simulations to evaluate the multi-year implications of new policy initiatives.

Some cities have found that a constant services budget requires an increase in the quantity of inputs employed. For example, "constant" police services may be taken to mean a constant number of policemen per 1,000 population, hence, an increase in police employment if population is growing. Cities annexing land area face an analogous problem as regards the need to increase the number of inputs employed to keep service levels constant. This raises the need for a more sophisticated projection model, but it also presents the opportunity for more effective linkage between the multi-year projections and the annual budget process.

Under this system the agency-level units responsible for preparing the annual budget are requested to consider the future budgetary impacts of changes such as (a) planned new capital projects that will affect operating and maintenance costs of the department; (b) higher level government mandates that are scheduled to come into effect during the forecast period; (c) demographic or economic changes that will affect departmental spending; and (d) policy changes scheduled to be implemented during the forecast period. In other words, the cost implications of departures from a constant services budget are estimated.

The cities of Dallas and San Antonio have developed a systematic approach to gathering such information.[6] The success in these cities is due to their recognition that the estimation of such impacts can be accomplished most effectively at the agency level. For example, in the case of new capital projects, the operating department is in the best position to estimate the completion date of the project as well as to cost out the amount of new manpower and non-labor costs needed to operate and maintain the facility. Operating agencies are also most likely to be aware of new, mandated services and can provide the best information on the incremental costs of these policies. Agency personnel are also in the best position to estimate effects of assumed changes in population size and composition on necessary spending levels.

Such procedures have obvious implications for the annual budgetary process. Most importantly, they allow the system to anticipate a new environment in which the budget will operate. While one would hope that a budget division would collect information on such future events as scheduled mandates and new needs, the existence of a formalized process that requires budgetary submissions to include these factors means the persons responsible for budget preparation are less likely to be surprised. Furthermore, costing out the fiscal effects of these future resource needs makes the process more effective than a simple statement such as "the new park will mean that additional maintenance personnel will have to be hired by the Parks Department."

In order to insure that the long-term forecasts of needs are realistically submitted and are not, for example, simply indicators that whatever the agency is spending today will be spent in subsequent years, a more formal linking of the annual budgetary process and multi-year forecasting techniques is necessary. That is, if a department knows in 1983 that its 1985 forecast entries will be used as its initial budgetary allocation when preparing the 1985 budget, a more serious approach to the long-term forecast is likely. This is the technique used in Dallas and San Antonio, where any annual budget request not included in the previous year's long-term forecast is scrutinized closely before being approved.[7] On the other hand, if the long-term forecast is to be useful, it must be more than a wish list. To guard against this, both the Texas cities, New York City, and the District of Columbia use central review of the long-term forecast submissions. This review, carried out by the same budget analysts who review annual submissions, not only imposes additional "honesty" on the agencies, but can inform the budget analysts of likely upcoming events.

In sum, long-term forecasting can markedly improve the annual budgeting process. By requiring agency heads to think of the longer term implications of today's decisions, they can be made to consider more carefully the true cost of each expenditure decision. This may be especially true when they can see in detail that a submission on today's budget request may decrease their flexibility in subsequent years.

Revenue forecasting and budget preparation

There are several ways in which jurisdictions might forecast revenues three to five years into the future. Some of these are not greatly different from what is currently used in many jurisdictions to produce revenue estimates for the annual budget; hence there is the possibility that the annual budget revenue estimates and the multi-year projections can be meshed. This coordination may take the form of simply using the multi-year forecast as one piece of information in determining the annual budget estimate, or by using the first year of the multi-year forecast directly.

In some cities, e.g., Kansas City, Missouri, the multi-year forecast is produced several months prior to the beginning of the fiscal year and cannot be used directly in the budget document.[8] There are also cities, e.g., Dallas, where the responsibility for producing the multi-year forecast has been placed in a unit other than that responsible for the budget document itself. Nevertheless, even in these cases the output of the multi-year forecast may be used as one piece of information to aid in deciding upon the specific estimated revenue to insert in the annual budget document.

In cases where econometric techniques are used to forecast revenues, the model may be useful to the budget preparer. For example, while it may be anticipated that a recession will adversely affect sales tax revenues, an econometrically estimated function can give a quantitative estimate of the magnitude of this effect. Otherwise it would be necessary to guess. Although the econometric estimate may be altered, the results from the statistical equation provide a good starting point. Such an approach has been taken in Dallas.

Where there is sufficient confidence in the multi-year forecasting model, its output may be used directly to derive the budget estimate. In both New Orleans and New York City the same forecasting equations for the economically sensitive revenues are used for the annual budget and the multi-year projections. Few jurisdictions would be willing to take a similar step in the absence of any history of accuracy, but several years of good experience with a model can be convincing to policy makers. Tables 1, 2, and 3 provide some perspective on the forecasting accuracy obtained in three different cities during the late 1970s and early 1980s.[9] Table 1 documents the one-year forecast errors found for the major economically sensitive tax revenue sources in New York City.[10] A forecasting model is put to a serious test in New York City, where the revenue sources include corporate and unincorporated business taxes and levies on financial institutions. Because of their cyclical sensitivity, these revenue sources are quite difficult to predict accurately. Five to ten percent error rates seem the rule in these three years, in part because the unanticipated inflation of the late 1970s played a major role in the underestimation of sales and income taxes. The recent prolonged recession, while it has not struck New York City as severely as many other cities, still resulted in an overly optimistic projection of sales taxes. Overall, the New York City model has projected annual revenues with a very low 3 to 4 percent error rate.

For New Orleans the forecast errors for 1979 are from two different forecasts: The first is based upon the multi-year forecast published in 1977 and the second upon that published in 1978 (Table 2). The 1977 forecast of 1979 revenues was considerably lower than the 1978 forecast, a result that can be attributed to unanticipated price rises. The downside error in the property tax was due primarily to new assessment procedures implemented prior to 1979. The overall error in the 1978 forecast was smaller because of the shorter time horizon. This pattern is likely to hold in any multi-year forecast, because additional information allows for more accurate projections of the exogenous variables to be used in the econometric equations. The New Orleans results make a strong case for using a multi-

Revenue source	Fiscal year 1977 Forecast	Actual	Percentage error*
General corporation tax	$ 480.1	$ 518.5	– 7.41
Financial tax	173.6	148.5	16.90
Unincorporated business tax	72.2	77.7	– 7.08
Utility tax	105.4	99.8	5.61
Sales tax	850.7	867.4	– 1.93
Personal income tax	674.3	722.9	– 6.72
Stock transfer tax	275.1	279.7	– 1.65
Total	2,631.4	2,714.5	– 3.06

	Fiscal year 1978		
General corporation tax	$ 519.2	$ 491.9	5.55
Financial tax	165.0	147.9	11.56
Unincorporated business tax	79.6	85.5	– 6.90
Utility tax	113.0	108.7	3.96
Sales tax	901.3	931.2	– 3.21
Personal income tax	741.9	802.0	– 7.49
Stock transfer tax	228.0	290.2	–21.43
Total	2,748.0	2,857.4	– 3.83

	Fiscal year 1982		
General corporation tax	$ 609.7	$ 698.4	–12.70
Financial tax	218.9	204.9	6.83
Unincorporated business tax	132.3	123.3	7.30
Utility tax	164.3	173.8	– 5.47
Sales tax	1,432.8	1,414.8	1.27
Personal income tax	1,109.3	1,159.4	– 4.32
Stock transfer tax	183.0	202.6	– 9.67
Total	3,850.3	3,977.2	– 3.19

*Percentage error $= \dfrac{\text{Forecast} - \text{Actual}}{\text{Actual}} \times 100$

Table 1. Forecasting accuracy for selected tax revenues in New York City, 1977, 1978, and 1982 ($ millions).

year forecasting model directly in revenue estimation for the annual budget. In 1979 the overall error rate for all revenues was only 0.11, and it increased to only 0.22 percent in 1980. Such levels of accuracy would be difficult to equal, even through the more commonly used judgmental techniques. This would seem to be a strong endorsement of the econometric approach.

Forecast errors from the City of San Antonio are shown in Table 3. San Antonio uses a combination of econometric and trend

Revenue source	1977 Forecast	1978 Forecast	1979 Actual	Percentage error* 1977 Forecast	1978 Forecast
Real and personal property tax	$ 8,767	$10,150	$10,288	-14.78	-1.34
Sales tax	52,412	58,044	57,250	- 8.45	1.39
Utility tax	5,201	6,039	5,626	- 7.55	7.34
Licenses and permits	16,699	18,427	19,001	-12.12	-3.02
Total	83,079	92,660	92,181	- 9.87	0.52

$$*\text{Percentage error} = \frac{\text{Forecast} - \text{Actual}}{\text{Actual}} \times 100$$

Table 2. Forecasting accuracy for selected tax revenues in New Orleans, 1979 ($ thousands).

analysis techniques to derive its long-term forecasts but does not use the model directly in projecting annual budgetary income. The three sources shown make up the bulk of San Antonio's general fund revenues. Two different forecasts are examined in the table—one made about halfway through the 1978 fiscal year and the other midway through the 1979 fiscal year. Projections for both FY 1979 and FY 1980 are shown. As one would anticipate, "forecasts" only six months into the future (the 1979 forecast made during the 1979 fiscal year) are extremely accurate. But the methods employed also show reasonably accurate projections 18 and 30 months into the fu-

1979 revenue sources	1978 Forecast	1979 Forecast	Actual	Percentage error* 1978 Forecast	1979 Forecast
Property tax	$31,681	$32,737	$32,905	- 3.72	- 0.51
Sales tax	27,217	26,269	26,244	3.71	0.10
Public service tax	37,898	39,390	38,881	- 2.53	1.31
1980 revenue sources					
Property tax	$32,094	$32,689	$39,964	-19.69	-18.20
Sales tax	31,027	29,762	29,987	3.47	- 0.75
Public service tax	39,827	41,971	48,700	-18.22	-13.82

$$*\text{Percentage error} = \frac{\text{Forecast} - \text{Actual}}{\text{Actual}} \times 100$$

Table 3. Accuracy of 1978 and 1979 forecasts of major tax revenues in San Antonio for 1979 and 1978 ($ thousands).

ture. Projections of San Antonio's general fund property tax revenues (shown in Table 3) are complicated by the fact that this tax must first be dedicated to provide coverage of any general obligation debt with the remainder flowing to the general fund. The 1980 forecast errors shown in Table 3 primarily reflect errors in overestimating the amount of general obligation debt service rather than structural errors in forecasting the property tax. Underestimation of public service revenues stems from the rapid increase in utility prices while the tax is tied to gross revenues. Again, however, more current forecasts were found to be more accurate than longer range projections.

Use of a multi-year forecast in the annual budget process

The most obvious policy use of a multi-year forecast arises when a revenue gap is projected. Even if the projected gap is several years into the future, the forecast has produced an "early-warning signal" that steps may have to be taken immediately to avoid the gap. Indeed, in this sense the forecast will never be accurate; i.e., it will lead to steps to erase the projected unfavorable outcome. It would not be uncommon for the multi-year projection results to lead to the following outcomes:

1. A capital project might be delayed or reduced in size because of the operation and maintenance expenditures implied for the current budget.
2. New programs might be denied to help accumulate a current surplus for use in future years where a more bleak fiscal position has been projected. For example, this might be an action taken as regards the phasing down of certain federal aid programs.
3. Pension, fringe benefit, and wage rate negotiations may be markedly influenced by demonstrations of long-run affordability.

In general, the advantage offered the annual budget process is more information about the prospects for the local fiscal environment. An especially important contribution from a systematic multi-year forecasting system, especially if it is computerized so that different scenarios may easily be tried, is that the longer range implications of alternative budget initiatives can be estimated before the budget is put into final form.[11]

A very good example of the use of multi-year forecasting to deal with the annual budget gap is in the procedures followed in New York City. As a part of their multi-year forecast, the kinds of alternative policies necessary to close the projected budget gap are shown explicitly. While the output from that forecast may not be identical to the ultimate cutback decisions made, it does show policy makers and the public the extent of the problem and gives an indication of the kinds of policy responses that will be necessary to insure that future deficits will not occur.[12]

The approach taken in New York has been replicated, and even expanded, in several cities which have developed multi-year forecasting models during the past few years. In its first multi-year forecast, Shreveport not only identified 31 specific measures necessary to close the projected 1982 budget gap, but also showed the net fiscal effect of these actions during the subsequent three years and identified and estimated the cost savings of 12 additional measures to be undertaken during 1983–1985.[13]

Two Texas jurisdictions, Dallas County and the City of Fort Worth, are also using their forecasts as a long-term strategy formulation device. In its 1982–1986 forecast, Fort Worth included several revenue and expenditure strategies designed to preclude a projected budget gap.[14] Similarly, Dallas County includes a lengthy discussion of specific strategies that could be undertaken either to yield cost savings or to generate additional revenues.[15]

On the revenue side of the budget there are specific policy decisions that can result directly from the multi-year forecast. Again, in the face of future revenue shortfalls, policy makers may decide that increases in tax rates or user fees and charges are justified. Not only will the models suggest the extent of the shortfall, but the more sophisticated models can be specified in a manner so that the revenue impacts of alternative rate adjustments can be estimated.

Finally, the multi-year forecast can provide an atmosphere for more rational budgeting. When policy makers can be shown the extent of the potential problems the jurisdiction will face within the next few years, they may be less willing to undertake expansionary policies that may come back to haunt them later. Furthermore, most models currently being used can be employed to show the extent to which the locality is at risk with respect to possible downturns in the national economy, increases in inflation, or political decisions that could be made at higher levels of government.[16] Recent concern about the fiscal implications of rampant inflation is obvious from a review of several forecasts produced within the past two years which show, as well, the sensitivity estimation potential of the multi-year models. For example, the cities of Dallas, San Antonio, and Vancouver each produced estimates of revenues and expenditures under alternative assumptions about price changes.[17] In a similar vein, Phoenix used a multi-year model in studying the impact of a state expenditure limitation law.[18] In this way budget makers could see the extent of the difference between what would likely have been spent and the upper limit of what the state of Arizona was mandating could be spent, thus providing them some perspective regarding the degree to which they would have to cut back in upcoming budgets. While sobering, when hard dollar estimates of the fiscal implications of locally uncontrollable events are put before policy makers, it provides a more realistic setting for budgetary decision.

Summary

The thesis of this article is that multi-year forecasting can be made an integral part of the overall financial management process of a jurisdiction and can be linked directly to the annual budgetary process. While the techniques are not complicated, forecasts of spending over the longer term can be used to prevent major budgetary surprises and, as well, can give department heads a longer time perspective on the requests made in preparation of the annual budget. Likewise, the forecasts from multi-year revenue models can be used directly in formulating annual budget estimates or, at the very least, can be used as additional information in finalizing these estimates. All of these uses can then feed into the final budget approval process. While the forecast is not a sufficient condition to avoid all future budgetary problems, it does aid in avoiding the common budget-making trap of being overly myopic on the consequences of current decisions.

1. These techniques are described in more detail in Roy Bahl and Larry Schroeder, "Forecasting Local Government Budgets," Occasional Paper No. 38, Metropolitan Studies Program, the Maxwell School (Syracuse, N.Y.: Syracuse University, 1979).

2. Larry Schroeder, Lee Madere, and Jerome Lomba, "Local Government Revenue and Expenditure Forecasting: New Orleans," Occasional Paper No. 52, Metropolitan Studies Program, the Maxwell School (Syracuse, N.Y.: Syracuse University, September 1981).

3. Roy Bahl, Larry Schroeder, Marla Share, and Anne Hoffman, "Local Government Revenue and Expenditure Forecasting: Washington, D.C.," Occasional Paper No. 51, Metropolitan Studies Program, the Maxwell School (Syracuse, N.Y.: Syracuse University, September 1981).

4. Roy Bahl, Larry Schroeder, and Kurt Zorn, "Local Government Revenue and Expenditure Forecasting: New York City," Occasional Paper No. 50, Metropolitan Studies Program, the Maxwell School (Syracuse, N.Y.: Syracuse University, September 1981).

5. Given their uncontrollable nature, transfer programs in both the District of Columbia and New York City are projected using a different technique. Case loads as well as unit costs are forecast, with the former usually linked to the economic assumptions that underlie the forecast.

6. See Roy Bahl, Larry Schroeder, and Kurt Zorn, "Local Government Revenue and Expenditure Forecasting: Dallas, Texas," Occasional Paper No. 49, Metropolitan Studies Program, the Maxwell School (Syracuse, N.Y.: Syracuse University, September 1981); and Roy Bahl, Larry Schroeder, and Marla Share, "Local Government Revenue and Expenditure Forecasting: San Antonio," Occasional Paper No. 48, Metropolitan

Studies Program, the Maxwell School (Syracuse, N.Y.: Syracuse University, September 1981).

7. Ibid.

8. Office of Budget and Systems, *Five-Year Financial Forecast, 1983–84 to 1987–88* (Kansas City, 1982).

9. Because of its special nature, the real property tax in New York City is not classified as an economically sensitive revenue source and is forecast using judgmental rather than econometric techniques.

10. A detailed examination of the accuracy of forecasting a single revenue source and how that accuracy has improved over time is contained in City of San Diego, Financial Management Department, "A Retrospective Look at the Success of Long-Range Revenue Forecasting" (San Diego, 1982).

·1. This is one use that has been made of the multi-year model implemented in the District of Columbia. See Bahl, Schroeder, Share, and Hoffman, "Local Government Revenue and Expenditure Forecasting: Washington, D.C."

ι2. See Bahl, Schroeder, and Zorn, "Local Government Revenue and Expenditure Forecasting: New York City."

ι3. City of Shreveport, *Multi-Year Forecast, 1981–1985* (Shreveport, 1981).

14. Office of Management Services, Fort Worth, Texas, *Long Range Financial Forecast, 1982 to 1986* (Fort Worth, 1981).

15. Dallas County, Texas, Office of Commissioners Court, *FY-82 Long Range Plan for Dallas County* (Dallas, 1982).

16. For an example of an analysis of this degree of risk within an intergovernmental setting, see Roy Bahl and Larry Schroeder, *Projecting and Planing State and Local Government Fiscal Activity in a Declining Region: The New York Case*, Monograph No. 5, Metropolitan Studies Program, the Maxwell School (Syracuse, N.Y.: Syracuse University, 1980).

17. Office of Management Services, Dallas, Texas, *Summary Long-Range Financial Projections: 1980–81 to 1984–85* (Dallas, 1981); Department of Budget and Research, San Antonio, Texas, *Long-Range Financial Forecast: Fiscal Years 1982–1987* (San Antonio, 1982); and City of Vancouver, Washington, *Five-Year Financial Forecast: 1983–1987* (Vancouver, 1982).

18. Management and Budget Department, Phoenix, Arizona, *Five-Year Forecast and City Options* (Phoenix, 1981).

Econometric Forecasting: Guidance for Local Revenue Forecasters

— C. Kurt Zorn

Historically, revenue estimation has been a crucial element in the local government financial management process. Short-run projections are common practice: all cities project revenues in preparing the annual budget and many predict monthly intake so as to more efficiently manage their cash position. There has been a growing concern with the ability to meet long-term debt obligations and pension commitments, to adequately maintain capital stock, to meet employee contract demands, and to continue support for existing programs. As these concerns have mounted, interest in multiyear (three to five years) budgetary forecasting has increased.

As interest in multiyear revenue forecasting has grown, so has the demand for information on how a local government can implement its own forecasting model. Documentation of the process used in various cities does exist, but many of the documents are intended primarily for internal use and thus contain little more than the specifics of the forecasting model—equations, relevant statistics, data, and forecasts.[1] More general information on the state of the art of local multiyear forecasting has appeared which describes, in a case study format, the techniques used by a number of large cities.[2] [See the preceding article.]

Unfortunately, access to documentation of techniques utilized by other jurisdictions does not appear to be a sufficient condition for the development of a multiyear revenue forecasting model. A study concluded that models specific to a jurisdiction, developed from scratch, will generally provide more accurate projections than a model which is borrowed from another jurisdiction.[3] Thus a

Reprinted with permission from the autumn 1982 issue of *Public Budgeting & Finance*.

municipality, in order to achieve the best results, will have to tailor any model to the local economy and revenue structure.

The econometric techniques used in the preparation of multiyear forecasts generally demand more sophisticated equipment (computer access) and more highly trained personnel (statistics background) than the best guess and time trend techniques commonly utilized for short-run projections.[4] Fulfillment of these resource requirements does not in itself guarantee good forecasts. The monumental task of constructing the forecast model remains—combining the available knowledge of the local economy, local revenue structure, and statistics to arrive at revenue forecasting equations.

This article provides guidance for local officials who are interested in the preparation of multiyear forecasts. It points out the problems that will be faced in the formulation and estimation of the forecasting model and provides solutions to these questions and problems.

What constitutes a good forecast?

Ideally, revenue forecasting will be done "in-house"—by employees of the local government. This is important since the accuracy of local revenue forecasts hinges on the forecaster's detailed knowledge of idiosyncracies in the data and of legal and administrative forces affecting revenue sources, and a good perception of how demographic and economic factors relate to these revenue sources.

Multiyear forecasts are most useful in assisting with gap analysis—determining the size of the gap between revenues and expenditures over the time horizon under examination. As a result, the local revenue forecaster will be concerned with point predictions which forecast a single value for each forecast period. Accuracy of the point forecasts is a logical goal if the predictions are to be used by the local government in its financial management process. If the forecasts prove to be accurate, they will gain stature and are more likely to become an integral part of the budget-making process.

Point forecasts may be either unconditional or conditional predictions. The former occurs when all explanatory variables are known with certainty in the forecast period, $t + 1$. For example, if it is hypothesized that sales tax revenues are a function of local personal income,

$$\hat{Y}_{t+1} = \hat{\alpha} + \hat{\beta} X_{t+1} \tag{1}$$

where

$\hat{Y}_{t+1}$ = the forecast of sales tax revenues in time period $t+1$
$\hat{\alpha}$ = the intercept
$\hat{\beta}$ = the coefficient of local personal income
X_{t+1} = the value of personal income in the $t+1$ time period

sales tax revenues can be forecast from equation 1. Unfortunately, the independent variable(s), in this case local personal income, is often not known for time period $t+1$. As a result, one must rely on a conditional forecast as represented by equation 2,

$$\hat{Y}_{t+1} = \hat{\alpha} + \hat{\beta}\hat{X}_{t+1} \qquad (2)$$

where

$\hat{X}_{t+1}$ = the forecast of local personal income.

Since the forecast of sales tax revenues, $\hat{Y}_{t+1}$, is now dependent on the forecast of local personal income, $\hat{X}_{t+1}$, it can be expected that the forecast obtained in equation 2 will be less accurate than that obtained from equation 1.

Accuracy of the forecasts can be determined through the use of forecast accuracy tests. A drawback to these tests is that they can only evaluate *ex post*—the forecaster must have actual values to compare to the predicted values—instead of *ex ante*. Once actual values are known, there are numerous tests which can be employed.[5] The mean absolute percentage error (MAPE) test

$$\text{MAPE} = \frac{\sum_{t=1}^{h} \frac{(A_t - F_t)}{A_t}}{h} \qquad (3)$$

where

A = actual
F = forecast
t = time period
h = number of periods in the forecast horizon

is superior for the local government interested in using forecasts for gap analysis. The MAPE allows the forecaster to choose the best forecast in terms of *ex post* accuracy and gain insight into the relative size of the forecast error, while the other tests provide a measure of accuracy but concern themselves with the absolute size of the forecast error. As a result, the forecaster using the MAPE can easily compare the errors from predicting different revenue sources. For example, a 5 percent error in predicting sales tax collections is comparable to a 5 percent error in predicting parking fines, while knowledge of a $1,000 error in predicting revenues from each source would not immediately indicate how good or bad the predictions are in relation to each other.

Specification of the model

The first, and probably most important, step in the forecasting process is the specification of the model. Failure to correctly identify the relationships among variables may lead to inaccurate forecasts and hinder the formulation of policy to respond to projected revenue gaps.

A priori economic theory is essential for identifying variables which affect revenue streams and suggesting the interactions among these variables. A familiarity with previous work, both theoretical and empirical, is therefore important to the local revenue forecaster.[6] But reliance on theory alone will not guarantee specification of the best forecasting model—theory must be combined with knowledge of the structure and administration of local revenues. A discussion of specification issues will clarify this point.

Timing   Once the appropriate causal variables have been chosen, the model builder must consider the time relationship among the variables, i.e., whether the independent variables should be lagged by one or more time periods.[7] This is because the dependent variable reacts to changes in some explanatory variables only after a period of time. Thus, the inclusion of lagged independent variables represents the less than instantaneous response of the dependent to the independent variable.

There are two main reasons for lagged independent variables. First, in very few instances do fiscal years and calendar years coincide. Revenues are reported on a fiscal year basis, while the majority of available independent variables are reported on a calendar year basis. Thus, the causal variables should be lagged by one time period.

Second, changes in demographic and economic variables do not always have an immediate effect on revenues. For example, an increase in income may not be immediately felt by consumers, and consumption patterns may be slow in changing. Thus, changes in sales tax revenues lag the income increase. Once again, a lag between the dependent and explanatory variable would be appropriate.

Functional form   Theory often fails to indicate the functional form for the estimating equations. A survey of local revenue forecasting models suggests that a simple linear functional form is appropriate for all revenue sources.[9] But both the linear and log-linear functional forms are used in estimating and forecasting state revenues, indicating that both functional forms should be considered by the local forecaster.[10] Lacking any clear choice between the two functional forms, the forecaster should determine which provides the most accurate forecasts.

Specification error   Specification error is common to local multiyear forecast models. It occurs when errors exist in the formulation of the regression equation. Data limitations and lack of theory restrict the forecaster's ability to formulate the ideal revenue forecasting equations. For example, a relevant variable may be excluded due to the absence of data, or the incorrect functional form may be used.

There is little that can be done about specification error, since it results from data and theory constraints. If specification error is present, it will affect the estimation of the relationships among the dependent and independent variables, but it will not affect the point forecasts. Thus, local revenue forecasters need not be totally discouraged by this problem because they will be able to prepare reasonable gap forecasts but will not get a true reading of the relative strength of the interactions among variables.

Data considerations
Many of the important problems in the specification and estimation of a forecasting model involve the availability of data. Data availability may result in too few observations and too few variables, thus contributing to specification error; those variables that are available oftentimes contain errors in measurement; and revenue data contain rate and base components which must be disaggregated in order to correctly estimate their relationship to demographic and economic variables.

Measurement error   The data used in the social sciences are seldom precise or exact. A variety of errors are introduced in the process of reporting and compiling data, and each will contribute to specification error. The three major sources of measurement error which the local revenue forecaster will encounter are estimation error, rounding error, and errors in computation of the data.

Estimation error arises because many of the demographic and economic variables are not measured on an annual basis, but instead estimated. For example, local population is measured every ten years during the national census, and the Bureau of the Census prepares estimates for the intervening years.[11] The systematic provision of revisions underscores the inexactness of these estimates.

Round-off error is a problem common to most data. This occurs when the data are expressed in other than singular units. It is not uncommon for large revenue sources, such as property taxes and sales taxes, to be expressed in thousand dollar units rather than dollar units. Also, it should be recognized that some error may appear due to computation of the revenue streams and the independent variables.

Variables used in local econometric revenue forecasting may be subject to measurement error. These measurement errors contribute to specification errors which do not affect the point forecasts, but, when the measurement error occurs in the independent variables, the power of the econometric model to shed light on the interaction among the revenue source and the demographic and economic variables is diminished. Unfortunately, there is little that the forecaster can do to avoid the problem.

Data cleaning   Since revenue forecasting relies on the use of time series data, the researcher should be concerned with the consistency of the data. Specifically, a historical revenue series contains both discretionary and automatic effects. The forecaster is interested in the variation in the revenue series due to automatic effects—variations due to changes in demographic and economic variables such as population, income, and inflation. Thus, it is desirable to clean the historical revenue series of discretionary changes in legal tax rates, in the base of revenue source, and in the administration of the revenue source.

Three methods have been proposed to clean revenue data—the data adjustment method, constant structure method, and rate variable approach.[12] The data adjustment method is not well suited for local revenue forecasting since it requires that information be available concerning the base of the revenue series. This is not always the case: for example, data on taxable consumption expenditures, the base for the local sales tax, are generally not available. Even if information on the revenue base is available, it may not be in a readily usable form. For instance, many local governments will have data on the assessed value of property, the base of the property tax, but the data will be disaggregated into many categories which are subject to different rates, exemptions, and exclusions. Thus, obtaining an overall property tax base figure can be time-consuming if not impossible.

The constant structure method is more useful to the local forecaster because it does not necessitate information on each tax base. As long as historical information about rates and yields is known, data which are commonly compiled on the local level, the base can be calculated

$$B_i = \frac{T_i}{r_i} \tag{4}$$

B_i = base of tax in year
T_i = tax collections in ith year
r_i = statutory rate in ith year.

Obviously, this method only cleans the data for rate effects.

A third method which can be used to clean the historical revenue series of discretionary changes entails introducing a dummy variable and/or rate variable into the estimating equation. The inclusion of a rate variable will account for the effect that rate changes have had on the revenue series over the years. The dummy variable is used to account for nonquantifiable discretionary changes, e.g., changes in assessment practices or changes in collection practices. Generally, a dummy variable is introduced for each identifiable legal and administrative change. Of course, a dummy variable can be used along with the constant structure method to encompass all nonautomatic effects.

There are drawbacks to the aforementioned methods. The constant structure method fails to allow for any feedback effects. A tax rate change can affect the size of the tax base, yet this cleaning method cannot quantify this effect. The major drawback in using the rate/dummy variable approach is the reduction in degrees of freedom in the estimation equation. Generally speaking, a degree of freedom is lost every time a parameter is estimated. Estimation of a model requires an adequate number of degrees of freedom (although there is no explicit rule of what an adequate number is). The local forecaster must realize the degrees of freedom are minimal when preparing a local forecast model, due to the short time series available for most local revenue data.

The choice of whether to use the constant structure or rate variable approach to clean the revenue series is not clearcut. Thus, both approaches should be tried to determine which provides the more accurate forecasts.

Data availability The availability of data is the most serious constraint on accurate forecasting of local government revenues. Although an econometric model should be based on economic theory, the application of theory is almost always restricted by the data.[13] Two main considerations must be kept in mind by the researcher: first, whether consistent historical series of the appropriate variables can be obtained, and second, whether accurate forecasts of the variables can be obtained (specifically forecasts of the independent variables, since multiyear forecasts will be conditional forecasts).

As a researcher becomes interested in smaller units of analysis, the problem of data availability usually increases. In the context of local revenue forecasting, the availability of data for possible independent variables decreases as the analyst moves from the federal to the state to the local level of government. For example, annual data on national personal income are readily available, yet there is no central source of annual personal income data for municipalities. Some local demographic and economic data are available from state and federal government agencies, but these are generally available only on an SMSA or county level. Occasionally a local planning agency will collect data on demographic and economic variables which can be used by the revenue forecaster. If the city is large enough, it may collect and compile its own data.

Generally the forecaster must rely on data collected by the federal government. As a result, specification error will be introduced, since many of the available variables are reported only on the county level.[14]

Forecasts of local independent variables are generally not available. Thus the local forecaster must prepare his or her own forecasts of the variables. One procedure which can be utilized entails basing local projections on more readily available national projections.[15] The historical relationship between the local variable, say population, and national population is estimated

$$Y_t = \alpha + \beta X_t + \epsilon_t \tag{5}$$

where

Y_t = local population
X_t = national population

and then forecasts of local population, $\hat{Y}_{t+1}$, are made by

$$\hat{Y}_{t+1} = \alpha + \beta \hat{X}_{t+1} \tag{6}$$

where

$\hat{X}_{t+1}$ = a projection of national population.

Obtaining forecasts in this manner assumes that the local variable responds directly to changes in the national variable. Obviously, this is not always the case.

Estimation

Once the local revenue forecasting model has been specified, the forecaster must estimate the model in order to determine whether the specified relationships between the dependent and independent variables are statistically significant. In the process of estimation, a number of issues can arise which the local revenue forecaster may need to be concerned with.[16]

Multicollinearity An estimation problem a local forecaster is likely to encounter is multicollinearity. Multicollinearity arises when there is correlation among the independent variables in the specified model.

There are three ways for the local revenue forecaster to identify the presence of this problem. First, if individual t-statistics indicate that few or none of the explanatory variables are significant, multicollinearity is indicated. Second, a large change in the coefficients when data are added (or deleted) and when variables are added indicates a collinearity problem. A third way of identifying harmful collinearity is when estimation provides "nonsense" results, e.g., signs on the explanatory variables which are contrary to economic theory.

A high degree of multicollinearity does not affect the point forecasts, but does affect the identification of causal relationships among the variables. If the local revenue forecaster is concerned solely with gap analysis, the degree of multicollinearity will not need to be reduced. But if the researcher also wants to identify the underlying relationships among the variables, he or she will need to reduce the degree of collinearity among the variables.

There are a number of ways to reduce the degree of multicollinearity. Ideally, the explanatory variables can be augmented with data which are not collinear. However, this is not likely to be a feasible alternative, due to data availability constraints. A more reasonable alternative would be to scale down the model to fit the available data. This implies that one or more of the highly correlated variables should be dropped. If the model is correctly specified, dropping variables could cause specification errors which are more harmful than multicollinearity. Toro-Vizcarrondo and Wallace suggest a criterion to test whether the introduction of a zero restriction (dropping a variable) makes sense in attempting to correct for multicollinearity.[17] Previous work has indicated that use of the mean square criterion can improve the identification of causal relationships and is a way for the local forecaster to reduce the degree of multicollinearity in the model.[18]

Autocorrelation   Autocorrelation occurs when observations are related over time (specifically, the regression disturbance term at one observation is related to the disturbance terms at other observations). Three reasons for the problem are commonly cited. First, there may be consistent error in measurement in one or more of the independent variables which results in the correlation of the measurement error component of the disturbances. Second, relevant variables may be excluded from the model and the disturbance term therefore reflects the excluded variables which are related over time. Third, there may be a shock in one time period whose effect does not wear off in the immediate time period. For example, the closing of a Chrysler assembly plant in Kokomo, Indiana, would affect the locality's total personal income over more than one time period, although without correcting for autocorrelation, the effect would be realized for only one time period in a forecasting model for Kokomo.

All three of the causes cited for autocorrelation are common to local revenue forecasting. Both the point forecasts and the reliability of the summary statistics resulting from model estimation will be affected by the presence of autocorrelation.[19] As a result, the forecaster will want to correct for autocorrelation to improve the point forecasts and to provide reliable summary statistics.

The Durbin-Watson test is the most widely used and accepted indicator of first-order autocorrelation and is a standard feature of most computer programs which perform regression analysis. One difficulty with this test is that standard Durbin-Watson tables generally cannot be used by the local forecaster because of the small sample size involved in local revenue forecasting. If this is the case, the forecaster should refer to tables prepared by Savin and White which cover extreme sample sizes.[20]

Once autocorrelation has been detected, the model builder must correct for it. A commonly used procedure is the Cochrane-Orcutt procedure which some statistical computer packages contain. The result will be reliable summary statistics and a value for the correlation coefficient which can then be used to adjust the forecasts of the revenue series, improving the point forecasts.[21]

Simultaneous equation bias The local revenue forecaster will generally be faced with a set of simultaneous equations rather than independent equations in his or her forecasting model. Due to the difficulty of considering the myriad feedback effects, independent equations are generally used in local forecasting modeling, resulting in the problem of simultaneous equation bias. The problem affects the point forecasts and makes the determination of the causal relationships very difficult. Although there are a number of techniques available to correct for the problem, it does not appear that their use will improve the forecasts or the identification of the causal relationships. The techniques that reduce the simultaneous problem tend to amplify any specification error, resulting in no overall gain.[22] Thus the local forecasters need not concern themselves with the simultaneous equations problem when setting up forecasting models.

Conclusion

Multiyear revenue forecasting is as much an art as a science. An essential element of preparing an econometric forecasting model of local revenues is familiarity with the locality's economic base and revenue sources. This enables the forecaster to better specify the forecasting model and better evaluate the reasonableness of the forecasts.

The local revenue forecaster faces a myriad of difficulties while attempting to econometrically forecast local revenues. Although some of the problems cannot be easily solved, the majority can be surmounted without difficulty, improving the point forecasts and the identification of the causal relationships between the dependent and independent variables.

1. See, for example, Lee Madere, *Municipal Budget Projections: Econometric Revenue Forecasting* (New Orleans: mimeographed, 1977); and Office of Management and Budget, *Six Year Revenue and Expenditure Forecasts, FY 1979-84* (San Diego County, 1978).

2. Case studies have been prepared by the Metropolitan Studies Program, The Maxwell School, Syracuse University (September 1981), for the following cities: Roy Bahl, Larry Schroeder, and Marla Share, "Local Government Revenue and Expenditure Forecasting: San Antonio," Occasional Paper No. 48; Roy Bahl, Larry Schroeder, and Kurt Zorn, "Local Government Revenue and Expenditure Forecasting: Dallas, Texas," Occasional Paper No. 49; Roy Bahl, Larry Schroeder, and Kurt Zorn, "Local Government Revenue and Expenditure Forecasting: New York City," Occasional Paper No. 50; Roy Bahl, Larry Schroeder, Marla Share, and Anne Hoffman, "Local Government Revenue and Expenditure Forecasting: Washington, D.C.," Occasional Paper No. 51; and Larry Schroeder, Lee Madere, and Jerome Lomba, "Local Government Revenue and Expenditure Forecasting: New Orleans," Occasional Paper No. 52.

3. Roy Bahl, Larry Schroeder, and Kurt Zorn, "Projecting Local Government Revenues: A Comparison of Models and Results," paper presented at the Southern Economic Association Meeting, 1980.

4. For a description of the alternative approaches, see Roy Bahl and Larry Schroeder, "Forecasting Local Government Budgets," Metropolitan Studies Program, Occasional Paper No. 38 (Syracuse, N.Y.: Syracuse University, 1979), pp. 10-17.

5. For a review of these tests, see Kurt Zorn, "The Effect of the Public Sector on an Urban Area's Structure and Form and the Multi-Year Forecasting of Its Revenues" (Ph.D. dissertation, Syracuse University, 1981), pp. VI 22-28.

6. Presently there is a limited amount of work in this area. Some of the work includes: Bahl and Schroeder, "Forecasting Budgets"; Bahl, Schroeder, and Zorn, "Dallas, Texas"; Bahl, Schroeder, and Zorn, "New York City"; Semoon Chang, "Municipal Revenue Forecasting," *Growth and Change*, Vol. 10 (October 1979), pp. 38-46; and Zorn, "The Effect of the Public Sector," pp. VI 27-37.

7. Most local revenue forecasting models fail to address the timing issue. New York City, an exception, utilizes lagged independent variables in its equations. Bahl, Schroeder, and Zorn, "New York City," pp. 37-51.

8. Ibid., pp. VI 35-36.

9. Dallas is the exception; however, its use of log transformations is not based on theory but instead on obtaining the highest coefficient of determination (R^2). Bahl, Schroeder, and Zorn, "Dallas, Texas," pp. 34-35.

10. Zorn, "The Effect of the Public Sector," pp. VI 35-37.

11. United States Department of Commerce, Bureau of the Census, *Current Population Reports, Population Estimates and Projections*, selected years (Washington, D.C.: U.S. Government Printing Office).

12. The data adjustment method is discussed in A. Prest, "The Sensitivity of the Yield of Personal Income Tax in the United Kingdom," *Economic Journal*, Vol. 72 (September 1962), pp. 576-596, and the constant structure method is discussed in R. Bahl, "Tax Revenue Forecasting in Developing Countries: A Conceptual Analysis," Metropolitan Studies Program (Syracuse, N.Y.: Syracuse University, unpublished, 1972). Details about all three methods can be found in Zorn, "The Effect of the Public Sector," pp. VI 52-57.

13. It is pointed out by Farrar and Glauber that data limitations instead of theoretical limitations are often responsible for underspecified (oversimplified) econometric models. D.E. Farrar and R.R. Glauber, "Multicollinearity in Regression Analysis: The Problem Revisited," *The Review of Economics and Statis-*

tics, Vol. 49 (February 1967), p. 94.

14. Specific details about data availability for local forecasting can be found in Zorn, "The Effect of the Public Sector," pp. VI 58–72.
15. This approach is utilized by New Orleans; see Schroeder, Madere, and Lomba. "New Orleans," p. 28.
16. These issues are not explicitly considered in most of the local revenue forecasting models currently in use.
17. The criterion suggested is the mean squared error criterion. It entails estimating the equation with all the explanatory variables and then estimating another equation which contains a zero restriction for those variables thought to be causing the multicollinearity. If the latter MSE is smaller, than the zero restrictions make sense. The authors stipulate that this criterion should only be used in well-specified models. C. Toro-Vizcarrondo and T.D. Wallace, "A Test of the Mean Square Error Criterion for Restrictions in Linear Regression," *Journal of the American Statistical Society,* Vol. 63 (June 1968), pp. 558–572.
18. Zorn, "The Effect of the Public Sector," pp. VII 38–41.
19. Ibid., pp. VI 82–84.
20. N.E. Savin and K.J. White, "The Durbin-Watson Test for Serial Correlation with Extreme Sample Sizes or Many Regressors," *Econometrica,* Vol. 45 (November 1977), pp. 1989–1996.
21. For more detail on procedures to correct for autocorrelation, see Zorn, "The Effect of the Public Sector," pp. VI 86–89.
22. Ibid., pp. VI 100–106.

Bibliography

Armstrong, J.S., *Long-Range Forecasting: From Crystal Ball to Computer* (New York: John Wiley and Sons, 1978).

Bahl, R., and Schroeder, L., "Forecasting Local Government Budgets" (Syracuse, N.Y.: Metropolitan Studies Program, Occasional Paper No. 38, 1979).

Chang, S., "Municipal Revenue Forecasting," *Growth and Change,* Vol. 10, No. 4 (October 1979), pp. 38–46.

Department of Budget and Research, *Long Range Financial Forecast FY 80–85* (San Antonio, Tex., 1979).

Financial Management Department, *Six Year Revenue and Expenditure Forecasts, 1979–1984* (San Diego, 1978).

Madere, L., *Municipal Budget Projections: Econometric Revenue Forecasting* (New Orleans: mimeographed, 1977).

Office of Management Services, *Long-Range Financial Plan 1978–79 to 1982–83* (Dallas, Tex.: mimeographed, 1979)

Office of the Mayor, *The City of New York Four-Year Financial Plan, Fiscal Years 1979–1982* (New York, 1978).

Pindyck, R.S., and Rubinfeld, D.L., *Econometric Models and Economic Forecasts* (New York: McGraw-Hill, 1976).

Zorn, C.K., "Local Government Revenue Forecasting: A Guide with an Application to Memphis, Tennessee" (Syracuse, N.Y.: Metropolitan Studies Program, Occasional Paper Series).

Ethical Dilemmas in Forecasting for Public Policy

Martin Wachs

Forecasts are part and parcel of policy making. Governments deploy military forces and construct weapons systems on the basis of forecasts of actions by potential future enemies. Transit systems, power plants, hospitals, and airports are constructed only after forecasts have demonstrated that a "need" exists for their services and that their costs are justified by expected benefits. Testimony before Congress advocating increased expenditures for housing or education is considered incomplete unless forecasts of future need are carefully detailed. Economic forecasts are so influential as to be the subject of national media coverage, and of evaluations of national monetary or employment policy by competing candidates for high office.

The requirement to prepare forecasts is written into law and government regulation. For example, highway networks built in American metropolitan areas have been based upon a "comprehensive, continuing, and cooperative" planning process, institutionalized by the Highway Act of 1964. This act was interpreted as requiring that highway plans be evaluated against a 20-year forecast of travel demand, with the 20-year forecast being updated periodically to ensure that the plans remain valid. The Urban Mass Transportation Administration requires that state and local governments submit "alternatives analyses" as part of requests for funds under its capital grants program. The analysis must show that the course of action for which funding is sought clearly constitutes a superior use of public funds in comparison with all reasonable alternatives.

Reprinted with permission from *Public Administration Review* © 1982 by The American Society for Public Administration, 1120 G Street, N.W., Suite 500, Washington, D.C. All rights reserved. The author gratefully acknowledges the support of a Rockefeller Foundation Humanities Grant, which made this study possible.

Guidelines for the program require, among other things, that cost
and patronage levels be forecast for each alternative. Similarly, airport authorities produce long-range forecasts of air traffic in their
regions to arrive at proposals for new facilities; metropolitan planning organizations base housing programs on forecasts; and national energy policy debates have been motivated by competing
forecasts of the demand for and availability of fuels.

Forecasts can be made by politicians, clairvoyants, philoso-
phers, or prophets. In policy making, however, forecasts taken seri-
ously for any practical purpose are likely to be produced by technical experts, and it is technical forecasting to which this study is
addressed. In a society influenced by technology and technique, prediction is accomplished by applications of standardized methods to
carefully collected files of information. Forecasts in most instances
are produced by manipulations of computers which are probably
understood by relatively few of the people who act on the basis of
the results. Forecasters are usually experts, serving as staff or consultants to those in decision-making positions. Public officials who
employ forecasts as the basis for action rarely comprehend all of the
mathematical procedures involved in the predictions. They are
likely to be unfamiliar with the data series employed and unaware
of the technical assumptions hidden under the cloak of expert judgment.

The political salience of many forecasts and the technical complexity of the forecasting process combine to create for the forecaster an important ethical dilemma. Forecasts which support the
advocacy of particular courses of action are often demanded by interest groups or public officials. Forecasters must rely upon so
many assumptions and judgmental procedures that it is usually
possible to adjust forecasts to the extent that they meet such demands. On the other hand, forecasters are likely to view themselves
as technical experts rather than politicians, loyal to supposedly objective criteria according to which their work is judged in technical
terms rather than political ones. Public policy heightens this dilemma by requiring through laws and regulations forecasts which
are supposedly technically objective and politically neutral, while
distributing political rewards to those whose forecasts prove their
positions most emphatically.

Consider a situation described by Peter Marcuse, who changed
the name of the community in which it occurred in order to avoid
embarrassing those involved:

In Oldport, the mayor retained a planning firm as consultant to develop
a comprehensive twenty-year plan for urban renewal, housing, schools,
and social service facilities. The planners' preliminary report projected
moderate population growth but a dramatic and continuing shift in

racial composition, with minority groups reaching a majority in twelve years. A black majority was predicted within five years in the public schools.

The mayor reacted strongly to the preliminary report. If these findings were released, they would become a self-fulfilling prophecy. All hope of preserving an integrated school system and maintaining stable mixed neighborhoods or developing an ethnically heterogeneous city with a strong residential base would disappear.

The planners were asked to review their figures. They agreed to use the lower range of their projections—minority dominance in the public schools after eight years and a majority in the city in sixteen. The mayor was not satisfied. He told the planners either to change the figures or to cut them out of the report. They refused, feeling they had bent their interpretation of fact as far as they could. Without a discussion of these facts, the balance of the report could not be professionally justified.

The mayor lashed out at them privately for professional arrogance, asked a professional on his own staff to rewrite the report without the projections, and ordered the consultants not to release or disclose their findings on race under any circumstances. The professional on the mayor's staff initially demurred from rewriting the report but ultimately complied. The consultants remained silent, completed the formal requirements of their contracts, and left. The mayor never used professional planning consultants again.[1]

Here we have in a nutshell the central ethical dilemma of forecasting. Those who use forecasts, prepare them, or critique them, invariably use the language of technical objectivity. A model used for prediction is assumed to be unbiased, a tool in the hands of a forecaster who is a technical expert rather than a decision maker—a scientist more than a politician. Yet, so many technical assumptions are required to make any forecast that the process can ultimately be quite subjective, while the consequences have great significance. By choosing particular data or mathematical forms, many a forecast can easily be changed to transform increases into decreases, growth into contraction, gain into loss. These transformations can produce rewards or remove threats for those who accomplish them; they can often be made to masquerade as technical details rather than value judgments; and the outcome is frequently unverifiable.

Little attention has been given in the field of public administration to the role which forecasting plays in decision making. Even less attention has been given in the education of policy makers and technical experts to the ethical dimensions of forecasting. Without pretending to prescribe appropriate courses of action for those engaged in forecasting, this article explores the nature of this dilemma. Its roots are sought in both the technical aspects of forecasting and the political uses to which forecasts are put. This explication of this dilemma should help forecasters recognize the volatile situations in which it appears, and to address it more effectively in the education of policy makers.

The inherent dilemma of circularity

The role of forecasts in policy making is fascinating largely because it always involves an inherent dilemma of circularity. The future is made by people, and is not beyond our control. But to choose wisely from among alternative actions we seek information about conditions which will form the context of those actions. We want to know what the future will be like so that we can act, yet actions will determine what the future will be, and may negate the forecast. Because of this circularity, rarely may the accuracy of a forecast made in the public policy arena be literally verified.

A forecast of dire future events is made for the purpose of bringing about actions to avert that future. Having taken action and thus avoided the gloomy prospect, we can never be sure that the forecast events would have happened in the absence of that action. For example, if responsible medical authorities forecast that a particular disease will reach epidemic proportions unless mass inoculations are undertaken, a prudent government would surely conduct an inoculation program before victims begin to expire. If they did so, an incorrect forecast—with no epidemic in the offing—would yield the same measurable result as a correct one. The accuracy of the forecast could only have been proven had no action been taken and had the epidemic come about. Prudent policy makers would surely avoid the possibility of proving such forecasts correct, largely because of the dangerous potential consequences of inaction. Unless a forecast is considered frivolous, the salience of its consequences may be more influential than the probable accuracy. The international attention given to the Club of Rome's forecast of world ecological disaster follows more from its tenebrous visions than from its probable accuracy.[2]

A forecast of growing demand for some service, facility, or commodity and its provision in response to the forecast, give rise to a similar dilemma. The demand which is later observed might have been "correctly" forecast, or it might have been instigated by the forecast and the action which it spurred. In past decades, for example, electric utilities foresaw enormous growth in the demand for electricity, and expanded their generating capacity accordingly. Later, having huge capacity, they advertised electric appliances, lowered the price of electricity to users of large quantities, and invented new uses for electricity. Do the earlier forecasters of great demand now have the right to claim that their forecasts were "accurate"? Only in a superficial sense were they correct. It is the intertwining of forecast and action which is more important than any mathematical measure of consistency between forecast and actual consumption of electricity. Such examples serve to illustrate that there can be no absolute criteria of accuracy in forecasting for public policy, and that the supposed accuracy of any forecast can nearly always arouse suspicion among skeptics. From the inherent dilemma of circularity there follow many questions for those who prepare forecasts for government agencies, and those who employ their forecasts.

Forecasts require numerous assumptions

Many authors have drawn a distinction between forecasts on the one hand, and projections or extrapolations on the other. A projection or extrapolation is merely a calculation of the likely consequences of mathematical relationships between variables. A simple population projection, for example, would extend in time the relationships among birth, death, and migration rates. A forecast is more than a projection, for it involves also committing oneself to the selection of particular values of the variables which are involved. Thus, a forecast of population requires first that certain birth, death, and migration rates be selected as those most likely to prevail, and secondly, projecting the consequences of the specific rates selected. Clearly, the estimation of appropriate future values for these rates is a much more challenging task than calculating their implications. Technical expertise, however, contributes far more to one's ability to do the calculations than it does to one's ability to form the appropriate assumptions about future values of the parameters.

In a complex society, policies set by one organization or institution are inherently dependent upon the actions of many others. The demand for automobiles, for example, depends partly upon decisions made in Detroit, but also upon international politics, current wage rates, residential preferences, investment programs in highways and transit, changes in economic and family roles of men and women, and many other underlying conditions. Health care, housing, energy, and educational programs all present challenges to understanding and forecasting which are equally complex. These intricate interrelationships among the areas of modern society make it difficult to isolate clear cause and effect sequences which would allow forecasting with confidence. This is why Michel Godet has observed: "Forecasting in the classic sense of the word is possible only when man, through his past actions, has overcommitted his future to such a degree that the outcome can only take one or two forms."[3] Unable and unwilling to exert tyrannical control over events, we instead make forecasts which are conditional upon many assumptions about the likely behavior of some factors, so that we can estimate probable variations in others. Even a simple projection involving relationships among five or six variables would yield an unmanageable range of combinations of future conditions unless some of the variables were constrained by assumptions about the limits of their future values.

Without assumptions, forecasting would be impossible. But assumptions can be self-serving, and in the end can dominate the outcome of the forecast. William Ascher studied the accuracy of forecasts made over a period of 50 years in the fields of population, economic, energy, transportation and technological forecasting. He concluded that "core assumptions" were more important determinants of the accuracy of any forecast than were any other factors:

The core assumptions underlying a forecast, which represent the forecaster's basic outlook on the context within which the specific forecasted trend develops, are the major determinants of forecast accuracy. Methodologies are basically the vehicles for determining the consequences or implications of core assumptions that have been chosen more or less independently of the specific methodologies. When the core assumptions are valid, the choice of methodology is either secondary or obvious. When the core assumptions fail to capture the reality of the future context, other factors such as methodology generally make little difference; they cannot "save" the forecast.[4]

Reliance on assumptions is heightened by the fact that forecasts are often necessarily based on historical trends in variables, yet archives of data on social systems frequently provide historical information for only one or two points in time. It is difficult to project a trend on the basis of few data points, but this is often done by assuming a particular mathematical form for a curve and "calibrating" the trendline on the basis of only one or two observations. On technical grounds it may be quite risky to project a trend forward some 10, 20, or 50 years if the trendline is based upon information extending backward in time only 10 or 15 years, yet this is frequently done for practical reasons.

Extending a trendline based upon inadequate evidence of a relationship between variables is often a manifestation of a problem in forecasting which Ascher refers to as "assumption drag," and which he considers to be "the source of some of the most drastic errors in forecasting."[5] Assumption drag consists of reliance upon old core assumptions, sometimes after they have been positively disproven. He shows, for example, that population forecasters working in the late 1930s and 1940s continued to assume declining birthrates into the fifties and sixties, although the assumption of declining birthrates had already been authoritatively invalidated. Similarly, feminists point out that, while the majority of married women are today in the work force, many predict future household and labor force characteristics on the assumption that the single-worker household will continue to be the norm.

Assumption drag is due, in large part, to the simple fact that it is often more appropriate to incorporate into a forecast an historical trend than it is to anticipate a future deviation from that trend. The forecaster who projects the continuation of past trends may risk criticism for failing to anticipate systemic changes. Conversely, the analyst who forecasts coming systemic changes always risks criticism for going out on a limb, following hunches, or departing from conventional wisdom or established practice. It is usually difficult to decide whether a recent deviation from a long-term trend is a temporary secular variation or a permanent change in the trendline. It may take many years to recognize a systemic change in a policy variable. Furthermore, most forecasters are specialists who use information produced by other specialists as raw materials for their work. A forecaster of transportation or electricity demand may know far less about demography than a population forecaster, but may rely upon population forecasts as a source of change in transportation or electricity usage. While up-to-date on the latest analyses in his or her own area of expertise, the transportation or electricity forecaster may have access only to published population analyses which are out of date, and may not know of newer theories or conclusions in that area of study.

For these several reasons, analysts often conclude that variables which have been stable will continue to be so during the period for which a forecast is being prepared. Forecasting models may even reflect an assumption of stability by omitting from the model a variable deemed to be stable and hence less influential than others which are more volatile. This can have disastrous consequences if the passage of time proves the assumption incorrect. Consider the elaborate set of models widely used to forecast highway traffic throughout the world. These models, involving hundreds of equations, have been institutionalized through the widespread availability of standardized computer packages. The forecast procedures have been in use for more than 20 years, and were developed at a time when gasoline was inexpensive and in ample supply. Thus, while the models are notable for their level of detail, they do not explicitly represent the price or availability of gasoline as determinants of travel. When the forecasting models were formalized, gasoline was so widely available and inexpensive that statistical associations between these variables and the frequency or duration of trips were difficult to identify. The decision to omit these factors seemed rational on technical grounds. With hindsight, having experienced large changes in the price and availability of fuel and consequent fluctuations in travel, we may certainly question the wisdom of omitting them. The omission illustrates Godet's contention that: "certain forecasting errors are explained by our tendency to look at the 'better lit' aspects of our problems. The light dazzles us and hides from us what lies behind it."[6]

We more often assume stability than discontinuity, so assumption drag introduces into forecasting a systematic tendency toward conservatism. The centrality of core assumptions in forecasting makes this a serious problem, although attempting to overcome the conservative bias often means adopting critical assumptions on the basis of little supporting evidence. This dilemma contributes to the ethical quandary which forecasters face, because the absence of evidence supporting assumptions can easily reduce forecasts to statements of advocacy.

Technical expertise in forecasting

Despite the fact that assumptions play a larger role in forecasting than do the methods which elaborate upon them, forecasters are usually drawn from the ranks of social scientists, engineers, and planners whose education and professional identity are based primarily upon technical methodological skills. They are likely to believe and promote the belief that forecasting is impossible without the use of computers, mathematical methods, and complex data sets.

Sophistication in the technique of forecasting is more apparent, however, than real. Computers are used because there is often a great deal of data: many variables, many units of analysis for each, several time periods. These conditions lead to the requirement for training and experience in mathematics, statistics, data manipulation, and computer programming. But together, such skills ensure no special perspective on the future, and there is relatively little theory derivable from the social sciences to help one arrive at reasonable core assumptions.

Most forecasts result from extrapolations and assumptions rather than theoretical models incorporating representations of causality. Curve fitting and statistical tests of association may be employed, but extending a quadratic polynomial 25 years beyond the present is disturbingly similar to sketching a simple line on graph paper if the extrapolation is based on goodness of fit rather than an understanding of the underlying phenomena. Mathematical finesse enables one to connect models in series with the outputs of one forming the inputs to others, but if the models are associative rather than causal, errors may multiply so rapidly that they quickly dominate the forecasts. For these reasons, the technical elegance of some forecasting models is an illusion, obfuscating the central importance of assumptions which require or utilize no special expertise.

It would seem obvious that complex social or environmental phenomena can be forecast best using models which capture their complexity by representing the causal chains which underlie them. Thus, a simple model, predicting crime rates or air pollution on the basis of one or two indicators, is likely to be inadequate because we know that crime and air pollution result from many factors working in concert. In technical terms, simplistic models of complex phenomena are likely to have large "specification errors"—they fail to represent the processes by which outcomes are actually determined. By adding complexity—linking larger numbers of variables in longer causal chains—more sophisticated forecasting models can be developed which would appear to promise better predictions.

But complex models raise other problems. As more and more variables are included in the mathematical representation of a social or technical process, more data are required to use such a model in the preparation of a forecast. Of course, every bit of data used in a model is subject to error, and as more variables are used these "measurement errors" tend to increase more rapidly than the number of variables employed. A tradeoff must be made. Simple models, involving few variables, minimize measurement errors at the expense of large errors of specification. Complex models, involving many variables and equations, may reduce errors of specification, but only at the price of rapidly escalating measurement errors. An "optimum" forecasting model would be designed to the level of complexity which would minimize the sum of errors of the two types, but for most real phenomena analysts have no way of actually estimating the magnitude of each kind of error. Many feel that forecasting models of social, economic, and environmental phenomena have been developed to such a level of complexity that measurement errors are multiplied dramatically.[7]

Complex models are attractive for tactical reasons. They appear to be sophisticated and for this reason lend credibility to the advice given by those who understand them. Their very complexity makes it difficult to criticize or question their validity. In reality, they may be no more valid than very simple forecasting models which require less technical expertise.

There is a dangerous impression that forecasting is nothing more than data processing and extrapolation. Often, prescribed steps are followed to get a result even though the connections among the variables may not be known to be causative. No matter how accurate the data used and whether or not the structure of the model is appropriate, the specificity of the results often make them more plausible and authoritative than they ought to be.[8]

The political uses of forecasts

Governments with limited resources to allocate, and citizens who rely upon public services and pay their costs, would seem on the surface to assume that forecasts of future need and cost are executed with objectivity. The complexity of pluralistic and technological societies, however, places many burdens upon those who prepare forecasts, which make objectivity difficult to attain. Public resource allocation is competitive in that the decision to fund a project in one jurisdiction may deprive another of a similar opportunity. Political influence, financial gain, jobs, and prestige all flow from "winning" competitions for public projects. Technical experts are often employed by agencies which advocate particular solutions to certain problems: nuclear vs. fossil fuel plants for power; highways vs. rapid transit for urban transportation, and so on. A forecaster might be in the employ of an engineering firm which received a small contract to estimate the need for a bridge. If the bridge is shown to be justified, additional consulting fees for design and engineering may produce hundreds of times the income derived from the preparation of the forecast itself. If the bridge is shown to be unnecessary, no further contracts may be awarded. In such settings, it is obvious that forecasters are under pressure to adjust their predictions for self-serving purposes.

This pressure is intensified by the issues mentioned earlier: (1) a forecast is inherently unverifiable; (2) the outcome of a forecasting exercise is to a great extent determined by its core assumptions; and (3) the activity of forecasting is technically complex, revealing to most users its results but not its mechanisms or assumptions. It is indeed difficult to withstand pressures to produce self-serving forecasts which are cloaked in the guise of technical objectivity. By politely agreeing to speak of forecasts as objective, planners, engineers, or economists who prepare them can maintain their self-respect and professional identity. Simultaneously, advocates of particular positions gain strength for their arguments by virtue of the supposedly "unbiased" technical analyses which they can cite. And politicians who finally make resource allocations calmly accept forecasts which confirm their particular preconceptions with far less critical review than those which do not. All three sets of actors—technical forecasting experts, advocates for a particular point of view, and politicians—gain by pretending that a forecast is an objective scientific statement, and gain more if it is also an effective statement of advocacy in a struggle for resources.

In keeping with the illusion of technical objectivity, when the passage of time has shown the vast majority of demand and cost forecasts for public services to have been inaccurate, critics generally have contended that "imperfect techniques" and "inadequate data" were the sources of the problems. Rarely has it been argued that forecasts have deliberately been designed to place certain projects in a favorable light and others at a disadvantage. Rarely has it been argued that the structure of governmental decision making makes such ethically troublesome uses of forecasts inevitable.

Consider, as an example, the well-known case of San Francisco's Bay Area Rapid Transit System (BART). Capital cost forecasts for the 71-mile system, which formed the basis for the 1962 bond issue election, amounted to $994 million in construction cost plus $70 million for rolling stock. The final capital cost is now actually estimated to have been in excess of $2.4 billion (deflated to 1962 dollars). Design changes contributed to the deviation from the initial estimate, but there is no doubt that the initial estimate of capital costs was simply too low. The cost estimates may have been deliberately kept unrealistically low for political reasons. The value of general obligation bonds that could be sold was limited to $792 million, 15 percent of the assessed valuation of the real property in the proposed district which for 1960–61 was $5.3 billion. It appears that the estimate of the construction cost was at least influenced by legal restrictions on the borrowing limit of the district.[9]

The example of BART illustrates an age-old problem in forecasting the demand for and the cost of public works. If demand for a water supply system, bridge, or port facility is overestimated and cost is underestimated, the benefits of the project can easily be made to seem to outweigh the costs. Once the decision to build the project has been made, and expenditures of public monies have taken place, the realization that initial cost estimates were too low will rarely kill the project. Somehow, more money will be found to finish it. This was well understood by Robert Moses, as he planned and built the parkways, bridges, and parks of New York City. His biographer, Robert A. Caro, has written:

"Once you sink that first stake," he would often say, "they'll never make you pull it up." ... If ends justified means, and if the important thing in building a project was to get it started, then any means that got it started were justified. Furnishing misleading information about it was justified; so was underestimating its costs.

Misleading and underestimating, in fact, might be the only way to get a project started. Since his projects were unprecedentedly vast, one of the biggest difficulties in getting them started was the fear of public officials ... that the state couldn't afford the projects (which) ... beneficial though they might be, would drain off a share of the state's wealth incommensurate with their benefits.

But what if you didn't tell the officials how much the projects would cost? What if you let the legislators know about only a fraction of what you knew would be the project's ultimate expense?

Once they had authorized that small initial expenditure and you had spent it, they would not be able to avoid giving you the rest when you asked for it. How could they? If they refused to give you the rest of the money, what they had given you would be wasted, and that would make them look bad in the eyes of the public. And if they said you had misled them, well, they were not supposed to be misled. If they had been misled, that would mean that they hadn't investigated the projects thoroughly, and had therefore been derelict in their own duty. The possibilities for a polite but effective form of political blackmail were endless."[10]

The situation described is indeed an ethical dilemma because of the ambiguity and competing allegiances inherent in forecasting. The forecaster, in all likelihood, was educated according to a tradition of scientific-technical rationality, having allegiance to a set of methods and techniques rather than to particular outcomes in a policy debate. It is necessary to make assumptions so that the techniques can produce useful forecasts, and reasonable assumptions are not necessarily a betrayal of a commitment to technical objectivity. The agency for which the forecaster works, however, has a commitment to certain programs or solutions and believes that they can be shown to be superior to others on the basis of reasonable criteria.

In addition to commitment to a body of tools and techniques, the forecaster must also have loyalty or responsibility to the agency which he or she serves, either as employee or consultant. The employee wishes to advance and wants to be considered both competent and cooperative by his or her superiors. The consultant wishes to be considered for future contracts. Rewards flow from effective service as an advocate for the interests clearly identified by the organization. Should the forecast be made on the basis of core assumptions which seem most favorable to the furtherance of the organization's goals? Forecasts often require so many assumptions that there is leeway to allow the forecaster to satisfy both organizational goals and technical criteria. Indeed, if he or she has become a "team player" and has internalized the goals of the agency, there may not even appear to be a conflict between the two loyalties. In cases where the forecaster is aware of the conflict, and where reasonable technical judgment may deliver forecasts which the agency would rather not hear about, the forecaster faces the problem of choosing between advocacy and objectivity. The rewards for advocacy are clear, while even the criteria for judging objectivity are ambiguous.

Dahl and Lindblom observed: "someone must control those who run the calculations and machines. Someone must control the controllers, etc. At every point there would be opportunities for attempting to feed into the calculator one's own preferences. Doubtless, pressure groups would organize for just such a purpose." [11] It is critically important that public administrators recognize the limits of technical forecasts. There are few ethical guideposts included in the education of professionals, the canons of professional societies, or the processes of public policy making to suggest how such choices should be made. The choices are personal and sometimes troublesome. Frequently, the options boil down to serving the agency or leaving its employ. Because the agency itself, and the political process in which it is embedded, continue to describe, respond to, and reward advocacy as if it were technically objective and neutral expertise, only the most sensitive of analysts would choose not to serve as advocate. The result is that many forecasts are statements of hope and intention, while analysts, agency boards, and politicians cooperatively maintain the fiction that they are value-free projections of trends. Few forecasters engage in blatant falsification in order to receive a commission or promotion. Many, however, are transformed in subtle steps from analyst to advocate by the situation in which they perform their work.

1. Peter Marcuse, "Professional Ethics and Beyond: Values in Planning," *Journal of the American Institute of Planners*, Vol. 42, No. 3 (July 1976), pp. 264–274.
2. Donella H. Meadows, Dennis L. Meadows, Jorgen Randers, and William W. Behrens, III, *The Limits to Growth: A Report for the Club of Rome's Project on the Predicament of Mankind*, Second Edition (New York: Universe Books, 1974).
3. Michel Godet, *The Crisis in Forecasting and the Emergence of the Prospective Approach* (New York and Oxford: Pergamon Press, 1979).
4. William Ascher, *Forecasting: An Appraisal for Policy-Makers and Planners* (Baltimore and London: Johns Hopkins University Press, 1978), p. 199.
5. Ibid., p. 202.
6. Michel Godet, *The Crisis in Forecasting and the Emergence of the Prospective Approach*, p. 15.
7. William Alonso, "Predicting Best with Imperfect Data," *Journal of the American Institute of Planners*, Vol. 34, No. 3 (July 1968), pp. 248–255.
8. Solomon Encel, Pauline K. Marstrand, and William Page, *The Art of Anticipation: Values and Methods in Forecasting* (London: Martin Robertson and Company, Ltd., 1975), p. 66.
9. Martin Wachs and James Ortner, "Capital Grants and Recurrent Subsidies: A Dilemma in American Transportation Policy," *Transportation*, Vol. 8 (1979), pp. 3–19.
10. Robert A. Caro, *The Power Broker: Robert Moses and the Fall of New York* (New York: Vintage Books, 1975), pp. 218–219.
11. Robert A. Dahl and Charles E. Lindblom, *Politics, Economics, and Welfare* (New York: Harper, 1953).

PART 5

Future
Revenue
Sources

Revenue Prospects in the Service Sector

Astrid E. Merget

No single generalization can summarize how diverse services will behave as state and local targets of taxation. Revenue productivity and stability depend on the kind, mix, and stage of development of service industries in a jurisdiction's economic base.

Revenue prospects in the principal industries of the service sector depend on three factors: the firm itself, its workers, and its consumers. Even at this more specific level, generalization must be cautious: revenue prospects vary within every class of services; even in a single firm, the economics of headquarters may differ greatly from those of the "plant" that produces and dispenses the services.

Our emphasis is on the yield (in relation to manufacturing) and its stability in relation to the tax base. We will not directly discuss distribution of tax burdens, dynamics of shifting, impact on locational choices, or tax competition, although occasional observations on these issues appear.

Services are grouped into four main categories: transportation, communications, and utilities (TCU); wholesale and retail trade; finance, insurance, and real estate (FIRE); and services.

Three key factors affect services as revenue producers: (1) their internal economies; (2) how they fit the current tax base; and (3) what revenue instruments tap them best.

Transportation, communications, and utilities

In the main, these industries facilitate the flow across markets of production, distribution, and consumption or use.

Reprinted with permission from *Where Will the Money Come From?* published by the Academy for State and Local Government, Washington, D.C., May 1986.

Economies Interindustry linkages are key. Not surprisingly, these industries are very cyclically sensitive; as other industries that move on the cycle decline, the demand to transport will slacken. There are exceptions. In the collection are utilities which in a sense can act like fixed capital assets: whether a firm operates at maximum capacity in the upturn or at reduced capacity in recession, it still needs lights and heat. Second, sectoral shifts grip these industries as well; trucking and air have freed distribution from rail alone, as the auto has altered the journey to work. Third, communications is the vanguard of transformation—changing technologically within itself as well as altering organization and production in other industries; despite sensitivity to the business cycle, these firms are buffered by their sectoral rise. Because all firms under TCU are capital-intensive, recession probably means relative decline not only as demand slackens but also as costly expansions or renovations are postponed.

Most TCU industries rely on a unionized workforce. Across occupational ranks of operatives and craftsmen, the wage structure bulges in the middle. In a number of cases, industrialization of the service sector is evident, removing some tasks from labor. This is true in railroads, trucking and utilities, where computers may serve up routes, schedules and inventories. Communications is still at an innovative stage compared to the standardization evident in transportation or utilities; although it sports a cadre of higher-paid professionals, as standardization advances that fraction may shrink.

For land use, TCU means networks. Since TCU services exist to connect markets, location tends to be decentralized with nodes as ports of intake or deposit. In rail and trucking this pattern obtains, but air and water transport differ. Air transportation concentrates in large airports located at major nodes, despite numerous small airports dotting the landscape. Water transport mostly depends on natural, not man-made, location. Utilities will take on a more residentiary pattern following homes and other markets. Most of the "network" stretching over vast spaces is land-intensive and crosses boundaries, but often need not occupy the highest-priced land at the center. Because they are often regarded as polluting, unesthetic, and disruptive, TCU are apt to be off-center except for the natural placement of a river or harbor or the traditional downtown rail depot, where the market is at the core. Decentralization of the economy as a whole fosters even greater dispersal of TCU.

Tax base A local jurisdiction is hard-pressed to extract revenues from these firms. Despite land and capital intensity, assessment is complex, for lines of transportation, pipes, communications, etc., straddle many jurisdictions; apportionment becomes an issue. Typically, the land-related elements get taxed by charging for easements and rights-of-way. Where transportation is public, it would be exempt. Non-land elements also defy classical assessment; instead of evaluating the worth of a truck, plane, or railcar, other methods of extracting revenues may be sought based on volume (e.g., weights of trucks, fuel consumed), on use or on rights of passage.

A distinction must be drawn between the headquarters and the sites of transporting or communicating activities. So far as these industries display a concentrated form of market organization— they are, in many cases, technologically sophisticated, high start-up-cost industries that span long distances—they will require major corporate complexes for planning, managing, and financing. Their location in the traditional office high-rise is likely to be on the pricey land of a major nodal city or in a metropolitan subcore. Headquarters figure as a prime target for property revenues.

The labor component, heavily tilted toward operatives and craftsmen, displays a large chunk of middle-income earners. Depending on their choice of residence, they are likely to be healthy supporters of a tax system: they can often afford modest yet substantial homes, solid foundations of a property tax on residences; they probably will amply contribute to sales and income taxes. As these industries industrialize, however, a more skewed income distribution may appear; then, only jurisdictions where headquarters attract highly-paid professionals and managers will realize added property yields as well as sales and income revenues.

Revenues   Revenue structures that can better tap these firms (as distinct from their workers) probably fall outside the conventional categories. They may be fuel taxes or use taxes or volume-based; they tie to the right of doing business. Taxing profits or income may be thorny, since the network nature of these enterprises transcends jurisdictional boundaries; many are already in the public or quasi-public domain. Even so, their presence or absence may be so strategically crucial to the placement of other economic enterprises that their poorer revenue potential as direct targets of taxation may be offset by how much they attract other firms. A jurisdiction is better off with them than without them. Chart 1 summarizes prospects for direct revenues from these firms.

Wholesale and retail trade
Wholesale and retail trade are similarly characterized by inter-industry linkage. These firms are the conduits to consumers and users.

Economies   They are prone to be cyclically sensitive, following the course of goods. Since distribution tends to become routinized as markets stabilize, these functions allow standardization. For retail,

Chart 1. Revenue prospects for TCU firms.

Revenue instruments	Revenue bases Firm	Workers	Users/ consumers
Traditional sources			
Income			
Personal	NA	Moderate	NA
Corporate	Those in the public domain are exempt Otherwise potentially high but cyclically sensitive	NA	NA
Sales			
Gross receipts	Potential for profit firms	NA	NA
Retail sales	NA	Moderate	Potentially high
Selected sales	NA	Moderate	Potentially high
Property			
Land	Problems in discovering	Moderate	NA
Structures	value and interjurisdictional overlap with networks	Moderate	NA
Other	High for corporate headquarters Could exploit special assessment	NA	NA
Non-traditional sources			
Franchise	Potentially high	NA	NA
License	Potentially high	NA	NA
Utilities	Potentially high	NA	NA
Volume-related to use	Potentially high	NA	Potentially high with pass-on from firm
Transaction not output-related	Potentially high in a V.A.T. form	NA	Potentially high with pass-on from firm
Special establishment (e.g., hotels)	Could levy special tax on a major facility like an airport or harbor	NA	Potentially high with pass-on from firm
In-kind contributions	Contributions from public or quasi-public entities	NA	NA
Right-of-way	Potentially high	NA	NA
Privilege	Potentially high	NA	NA

where tastes and preferences vary, some measure of individualization and innovation exists. New communications that facilitate distribution; decentralization of transportation; cheaper land for storage outside central cities; the need to cut costly labor; the advent of robots—all have prompted some measure of decentralization for wholesaling. The extent might be regarded as off-center, since wholesalers need to be near market outlets of production and consumption. They are likely to consume a good deal of land on moderately-priced sites.

Tax base   They are apt to be solid targets for property taxation; to the degree that machines and equipment come to substitute for labor, these firms might become even more valuable objects of property taxation. Despite their cyclical proclivity—at least in the short run—land, machines, and equipment are fairly stable components; only postponing expansion may have a depressing effect on property receipts.

Workers in wholesale trade vary: managers pull up income levels; operatives unionized at mid-levels and sales workers push down incomes. Overall direction of wages tends to be fairly good. As workers buy homes and become property tax contributors, and as wage earners become consumers who pay sales and income taxes, the wholesale industry figures positively, but somewhat unstably due to cyclical sensitivity. Yields from the firms themselves fluctuate as profits rise or fall.

Revenues   Chart 2 sketches some revenue prospects for wholesale-trade firms. Relative to retail firms, these offer more promising tax potentials—themselves as objects, their workers, and their users. Their strategic role in market networks makes them candidates for taxes targeted to transactions.

Economies   Retail establishments look quite different. Although alike in interindustry linkage, cyclical proclivity, and potential for greater technology and standardization, they are distinguishable from wholesaling. Because they must locate near markets of final consumption as residentiary in nature, they are relatively dispersed. They cluster around population concentrations. They may locate in costly downtowns, often in status sites; some, such as the all-purpose department store, may consume large chunks of land. Others may gather in suburban malls, absorbing large tracts of relatively cheap land compared to the core city but rising in value with the outward migration of decentralizing economies. Still others may group at smaller scales and cheaper locations serving more distinct residences. Establishment size may vary, conditioned by the market, but more centralization appears as smaller firms are brought under the aegis of larger corporations. The locational preference of the corporate headquarters as distinct from individual retail places may also be the expensive corporate complex because of planning, finance, and advertising requirements.

Tax base   No single generalization comprehends retail's prospects for the property tax. To the extent retail establishments are labor-

Chart 2. Revenue prospects for wholesale trade firms.

	Revenue bases		
Revenue instruments	Firm	Workers	Users/consumers
Traditional sources			
Income			
Personal	NA	High for managers Moderate for operatives Low for sales workers	NA
Corporate	Potentially high but cyclically sensitive	NA	NA
Sales	Potentially high but cyclically sensitive	NA	NA
Gross receipts	Potentially high	NA	NA
Retail sales	NA	High for managers Moderate for operatives Low for sales workers	Some potential
Selected sales	NA	Same as above	Potentially high
Property			
Land	Moderate to high	High for managers Moderate for operatives Low for sales workers	NA
Structures	Moderate to high	Same as above	NA
Other (equipment)	Moderate to high	NA	NA
Non-traditional sources			
Franchise	Potentially high	NA	NA
License	NA	NA	NA
Utilities	NA	NA	NA
Volume-related to use	NA	NA	NA
Transaction not output-related	Potentially high	NA	Potentially high if pass-on from firm
Special establishment (e.g., hotels)	Potentially high	NA	NA
In-kind contributions	NA	NA	NA
Right-of-way	NA	NA	NA
Privilege	Potentially high	NA	NA

intensive, allowing some technology in computerizing sales and inventories, yield will depend primarily on the amount and cost of their land and structures. The picture then varies with type and size of establishment.

The rise of the mail-order house presents a peculiar problem for retailers. Their location was auspicious for sales tax revenues because volume generated receipts and retailers acted as collectors. Tax policies tailored to the sales tax and gross receipts make eminent sense for jurisdictions with many retail outlets. But catalog buying offers a convenient way for consumers to escape the sales tax and for retailers to thwart the "use" tax translation while minimizing property taxes. This trend is likely to prompt state-local officials to seek a reinterpretation of earlier rulings by the U.S. Supreme Court. For states with interconnected economies, tax cooperation may result, or states and localities may have to find alternative means of extracting dollars from mail-order establishments.

The retail labor force contains large fractions of sales and service workers, whose wages peg them at the low end of the income scale in unprotected positions. As objects of sales and income taxes, their earnings and spending do not promise high yields.

Because retail firms follow shifts in residentiary population and absorb many part-time workers, these firms are not stationary unless they have large sunk costs.

Revenues   Chart 3 summarizes revenue prospects for retail establishments. These firms play a strategic role of attracting and collecting sales revenue for jurisdictions. The firms themselves vary in revenue potential based on their size and site selection. Transaction-related taxes or privilege taxes could probably tap them better. Regardless of size, low wages of retail workers depress the revenue employees could contribute under income, sales, and property taxes.

Finance, insurance and real estate

These industries are difficult to characterize in output and connection with other industries. What they produce principally supports other activities.

Economies   Financial institutions make funds available to permit transactions and investments; their linkage to other industries and consumers is paramount. The same is true of insurance companies. Real estate firms may indeed deal in tangible outputs like land and structures, but the production "processes" of these services typically turn on a decision or judgment to lend, insure, or sell. Therefore, the collection and analysis of information are central activities. With telecommunications, a growing share of routine informational processes relies on machinery. Even so, these firms are largely labor-intensive because decisions require individualized judgment.

The interdependence of these firms makes them feel cyclical swings. Banking, as a case in point, may somewhat ride out the cycle because firms as clients still need to meet their financial obliga-

Chart 3. Revenue prospects for retail trade firms.

Revenue instruments	Revenue bases		
	Firm	Workers	Users/ consumers
Traditional sources			
Income			
Personal	NA	Low	NA
Corporate	Varies with size of firm and is cyclically sensitive	NA	NA
Sales			
Gross receipts	Potentially high	NA	NA
Retail sales	NA	Low	High
Selected sales	NA	Low	High
Property			
Land	From high to low varying with size of firm	Low	NA
Structures	From high to low varying with size of firm	Low	NA
Other (equipment)	Low	NA	NA
Non-traditional sources			
Franchise	Potentially high	NA	NA
License	NA	NA	NA
Utilities	NA	NA	NA
Volume-related to use	NA	NA	NA
Transaction not output-related	Potentially high	NA	Potentially high if pass-on from firm
Special establish-ment (e.g., hotels)	NA	NA	NA
In-kind contributions	NA	NA	NA
Right-of-way	NA	NA	NA
Privilege	Potentially high	NA	NA

tions; their new investments may be delayed in a downturn, however, so lending may lag. Real estate is particularly sensitive because recessions delay costly long-term commitments. As tax bases, these firms, although enduring and essential elements of a community's economic base, may rise and fall in activity with the cycle's vicissitudes. Deregulation of the banking industry has added further turbulence.

Tax base Despite new currents, the presence of financial, insurance, and real estate institutions seems auspicious for state-local tax policy. Regarding the property tax, while these firms do not consume large chunks of land and while they foster vertical development, they tend to choose expensive land. The small-town banks or branch locations tend to occupy prominent lots on downtown corners, as their big-city counterparts occupy expensive towers. Even this landscape is changing somewhat: automated banking permits moving to many, often less expensive, sites. In banking, automation sharpens the separation between sites for routine and nonroutine business. There is evidence of this in insurance with standardized, prepackaged policies. In real estate, telecommunications facilitate information flow, but eventually the choice to buy is time-consuming and labor-intensive.

All these firms in various degrees clearly exemplify the peculiarity of service industries today: The market may limit the scale of establishments dispensing a service, but firms are becoming more often large and centralized. With respect to location, the distinction between headquarters and service places is wide. Locations hosting headquarters will gain: property taxes will reap dividends from expensive locations; income taxes will be sustained by high professional salaries; and sales taxes will realize the benefits of higher-priced consumption, as may taxes on residential property. Jurisdictions housing these enterprises have often inventively tailored taxes to tap into stock-transfers, real estate sales, etc. When transactions spill over boundaries, a knotty new problem for the corporate income tax is how much to exact from headquarters compared to other divisions.

Revenues For jurisdictions that do not attract corporate complexes, revenue prospects may not be great. These firms have come to display the two-part wage policies that define so much of the service sector. Clerical components coupled with dispersed establishments and decentralization of backroom operations signify poor revenue prospects. Lower wages, smaller and cheaper sites, greater prospects for mobility: all portend poorer returns on property, sales, and income taxes.

Chart 4 sketches some of the revenue prospects for these firms. Capturing much of their revenue potential means amplifying the sales tax to comprehend their transactional activities, either on the firm as a gross receipts tax or on the consumer/user as an expanded retail or selected sales tax. Other possibilities include specialized taxes geared to the firm, such as franchise and privilege taxes or taxes pegged to professionals such as licenses to sell real estate or insurance.

Services

Generalizations across this group are difficult, since the firms appear so disparate, particularly in profitability. Possible commonalities include: the near absence of tangible outputs; closeness of the

Chart 4. Revenue prospects for FIRE firms.

Revenue instruments	Firm	Workers	Users/consumers
	Revenue bases		
Traditional sources			
Income			
Personal	NA	High for managers but increasingly lower with office clericals, non-office clericals and sales workers	NA
Corporate	Potentially high but cyclically sensitive	NA	NA
Sales			
Gross receipts	Potentially high	NA	NA
Retail sales	NA	High for managers but increasingly lower for other workers	Potentially high if extended to personal and business services
Selected sales	NA	Same as above	Same as above
Property			
Land	High in value, not quantity, for headquarters but increasingly lower with dispersion	High for managers but increasingly lower for other workers	NA
Structures	Same as above	Same as above	NA
Other (equipment)	Some potential with automation	NA	NA
Non-traditional sources			
Franchise	Potentially high	NA	NA
License	Potentially high	NA	NA
Utilities	NA	NA	NA
Volume-related to use	Potentially high on stock transfer, loans, insurance policies, real estate	NA	Could be captured through transaction-related taxes
Transaction not output-related			
Special establishment (e.g., hotels)	NA	NA	NA
In-kind contributions	NA	NA	NA
Right-of-way	NA	NA	NA
Privilege	Potentially high	NA	NA

service to final consumption as distinct from linkages to other outputs; labor intensity and low technology; and their personalized, individualized nature. Despite this, some evidence appears of routine and standardized operations that allow industrialization. Hotels are a case in point: Hilton, Marriott, and similar large-scale corporations operate through a complex web of dispersed establishments; while each may adapt style and quality to a localized market, service is essentially standardized. Still, opportunities exist for single enterprises with unique services patterned to a peculiar market. Industrialization also appears in personal services, as larger corporations offer housekeeping and hairdressing through chains; individual enterprises remain numerous. Auto repairs are probably most standardized of all, since they spring up around a "good" (the auto) rather than the idiosyncrasies of people.

All these services share a "residentiary" nature: they concentrate around markets, where consumers live and work. These establishments mirror the locational tendencies of others that reflect choice of residence and economic investment. Business and legal services, and to some degree hotels, tend to follow other firms—agglomerating in the corporate complex or dispersing in decentralized production plants. Hotels also come to leisure sites, where natural beauty or man-made attractions act as magnets: wilderness or golf courses. In contrast, personal services, auto services, health services, social services, education, museums and membership organizations disperse around clusters of residences. Exceptions include major medical centers, large research universities and sophisticated museums, which collect in centers and themselves attract other firms.

With some exceptions these services are less sensitive to the business cycle. Despite declining incomes in a recession, people are unlikely to cut back essentials such as health care and education; indeed, during a downturn the demand for social services is likely to rise. However, amenity services such as tourism, leisure and the arts will suffer. Business and legal services connected to productive activity may well decline.

These establishments are probably least likely candidates for revenue. A substantial share escape taxation under the property or corporate profits tax because they are nonprofit or public. Health services, education, social services, museums and membership organizations fall into these categories, though some make in-kind contributions to public service costs. To the degree that these services cluster around groups of people or are magnets, large shares of a jurisdiction's tax base may be exempt. Yet, with the exception of the large plants of major universities and hospitals, most individual establishments do not consume vast acreage.

Workers in these nonprofit or public institutions do not necessarily earn enough to become prosperous contributors to sales or personal income taxes. While health professionals earn sizeable incomes, most employees are in low-paying positions; the same is true for social services. Museums and membership organizations rely heavily on volunteers. Education engages a large number of professionals who earn at least mid-to-high incomes, often sheltered through unions and civil service. Cutbacks in the state-local sector and the declining birthrate, however, threaten this segment of services.

Across more profit-oriented segments, revenue prospects are mixed. Hotels—whether concentrated in economic nodes or free-standing leisure centers—may absorb sizeable, expensive land and yield well on property taxation. But they are likely to be buffeted by the business cycle, which may not show in property-tax yields but is likely to register in returns on corporate profits and specialized taxes targeted to users (e.g., hotel taxes). Furthermore, workers in these establishments are not generous givers to the sales or income tax: these firms have many low-skilled, part-time, unsheltered service workers. Their poor salaries translate into less valuable housing and lower property tax returns. One potential object of taxation for sales and/or special-use taxes are, of course, patrons, but yields are likely to be volatile over the cycle.

Business and legal establishments may connote the single professional in a solely owned business—earning a substantial salary, sheltered by occupational status, and occupying costly, prestigious space. But even these firms are centralizing in organization and clustering in corporate complexes. As fragments of basic service functions become more routine and information technology alters work, these enterprises are enlisting many lower-paid nonprofessionals.

Services do not need much land, but it may be very expensive. Value rather than quantity may mean healthy property taxes. Both legal and business services now rely more on the modern technology of telecommunications; yet problems abound with the discovery of value and the tendency to lease, not purchase. While service professionals may purchase or rent expensive housing, the large number of office clericals do not. Similarly, the professionals can be prime prospects for sales and income revenues; lower incomes of office clericals mean lower yields.

These firms could be affluent supporters of corporate profits, but their organization typically shifts taxes to individuals. As partnerships or sole proprietors, lawyers, doctors, and accountants face the personal income tax. For many local jurisdictions, which may not reap great property tax benefits from these firms and whose sales tax loses if it omits personal services, taxation of professionals is a possibility. Another indirect avenue to revenues may be taxes on the privilege of doing business or on gross receipts. Another tax may be use or transaction related: based on the legal value of a settlement or other proceedings, or the accounting value of an audit, a charge could be imposed. Most states, and especially localities, have not begun to fully exploit this segment of services.

Auto repairs tend to consume more land and rely on equipment. Their space needs dictate off-center locations near population clusters. They amply contribute to the property tax. As corporations, their profits can be captured under state corporate taxes, but if organized as partnerships or sole proprietors, only the personal income tax obtains. A number of these firms may be subject to a franchise tax as well. Operatives or technicians are inclined to earn moderate to middle incomes and hence be relatively stable sources of income and sales taxes. Users of these services can be easily comprehended by a sales levy on the dollar amount of service.

A number of these services (especially medical, legal, business, personal, and even auto repairs) easily slip into the so-called underground economy. Services can be rendered in-kind with no recorded financial exchange to claim as income or value.

Licenses are also potential tax prospects especially where professional skills are essential to practice. Certifications or permits to practice can cover a range of these establishments.

Charts 5 and 6 sort out some revenue possibilities by breaking apart the array of services according to their profit positions. In these groupings "other" revenue sources figure prominently.

Revenue strategies for the future

Simply scrambling for added revenues from service enterprises may indeed be counterproductive for jurisdictions. Tax burdens may deflect industries and firms and nurture an unfavorable business climate; redistributing tax burdens could unleash taxpayer antagonism and prove even more inequitable.

The implicit message for state-local policymakers is that many economic attributes of the service industry will not translate into revenues to offset losses in manufacturing, even if there is no job loss in a jurisdiction. This is especially true of jurisdictions that contain services characterized by:

1. High/low wage structures, with many employees in lower-paid ranks, which tend to be growing.
2. Less expensive land requirements.
3. Low levels of technology.
4. More advanced stages of development, where industrialization may bring larger scale but cost-cutting reduces labor and disperses to cheaper sites.

In designing strategies for economic development, simply securing service firms won't do. Labor, land, and capital ingredients; locational requirements; stage of development; cyclical sensitivity— all these are key, or the short-run dividends of capturing new firms and workers dissipate into long-term drags or decline in the revenue base.

(Text continues on page 172.)

Chart 5. Revenue prospects for services—hotels, etc.

Revenue instruments	Revenue bases		
	Firm	Workers	Users/consumers
Traditional sources			
Income			
Personal	Potentially high if organized as sole proprietors or partnerships; cyclically sensitive	High for professionals but very low for service workers, clericals, etc.	NA
Corporate	Potentially high if organized as corporations; cyclically sensitive	NA	NA
Sales			
Gross receipts	Potentially high	NA	NA
Retail sales	NA	High for professionals but low for service workers	Potentially high if levied on services
Selected sales	NA	Same as above	Same as above
Property			
Land	High values for headquarters, large-scale and status sites but increasingly lower for small, dispersed sites	High for professionals only and low for service workers	NA
Structures	Same as above	Same as above	NA
Other (equipment)	Some potential with automation	NA	NA
Non-traditional sources			
Franchise	Potentially high	NA	NA
License/ certification/ permits	Potentially high	Potentially high	NA
Utilities	NA	NA	NA
Volume-related to use	Potentially high if extended to transactions like filing fees	NA	Potentially high if related to service "inputs" (e.g. hours of service)
Transaction not output-related			
Special establish-ment (e.g., hotels)	Potentially high	NA	NA
In-kind contributions	NA	NA	NA
Right-of-way	NA	NA	NA
Privilege	Potentially high	NA	NA

Chart 6. Revenue prospects for services—health, etc.

Revenue instruments	Firm	Workers	Users/consumers
	Revenue bases		
Traditional sources			
Income			
Personal	NA	High for professionals but low for service workers; moderate for education	NA
Corporate	Probably exempt	NA	
Sales			
Gross receipts	Probably exempt	NA	NA
Retail sales	NA	High for professionals but low for service workers	Potentially high if expanded to services
Selected sales	NA	Same as above	Same as above
Property			
Land	Probably exempt	High for professionals, low for service workers; moderate for education	NA
Structures	Same as above	Same as above	NA
Other (equipment)	Same as above	NA	NA
Non-traditional sources			
Franchise	NA	NA	NA
License/ certification/ permits	Potentially high	Potentially high	NA
Utilities	NA	NA	NA
Volume-related to use	NA	NA	Potentially high if related to service "inputs"
Transaction not output-related			
Special establish- ment (e.g., hotels)	NA	NA	NA
In-kind contributions	Potentially high	NA	NA
Right-of-way	NA	NA	NA
Privilege	Some possibility	NA	NA

Scrutinized for revenue potential as tax bases for traditional instruments, many service industries do not look as robust as their manufacturing counterparts.

Fiscal futures

The economics of the service industries at this stage of development urge a strategy of greater revenue diversification and tax tailoring. Income and property taxes are most vulnerable to revenue losses from base changes due to industrial transformation, except in jurisdictions that house the corporate complex of high-salaried professionals and status-value sites. The sales tax could be enriched by expanding coverage to new classes of personal and business services. The ripest area for development lies in nontraditional types of revenue, targeted to service firms and their users or consumers.

Trends in state-local revenue now indicate this direction of change. Diversification has been occurring for complex reasons beyond the structural transformation. Added revenues must be found to circumvent tax limitations and/or to make up for short-falls in federal aid. Like any revenue strategy, diversification has potentially great problems. Broadening the sales tax or diversifying other sources could skew tax burdens regressively; it could further disgruntle taxpayers through more "nuisance" taxes; and service establishments may be driven away.

Resolving these perennial issues of elasticity, burden, and competition requires a good deal more knowledge than we now have about the economics of service industries and their implications for state-local revenue. The present codes used by national data sources inhibit analysis. We also need detailed studies of the service sector's inputs, technology, interindustry linkages, industrialization, and scale. With no comprehensive data base, the only instrument remains case studies on a disaggregated industry and state-local basis to catch relationships between the economic attributes of service firms and their revenue potentials.

Paying the Piper: New Ways to Pay for Public Infrastructure

California Office of Planning and Research

This article describes the principal methods that a local government might use to raise money for the public facilities that it needs, especially in order to serve new development. It passes quickly over the standard, traditional ways of using traditional methods to finance traditional things. There is ample guidance around on those. It concentrates instead on the hard-to-pay-for facilities, and on innovative approaches to paying for them, and for their operation and maintenance. It is intended to be provocative, suggestive, and exploratory. Local governments brazen enough to try some of the approaches described here might be sued (but with a reasonable chance of being upheld); elected officials proposing them can sometimes expect opposition. Paying for public facilities in California just now is a political, legal, philosophical quagmire. It is also absolutely essential.

New development in particular doesn't come cheaply, from a local government's point of view. It needs streets, sewers, storm drains, libraries, fire stations, police cars, water mains, and an astonishing amount of other publicly provided structures, machines, and people. All these things cost. It takes a fair amount of money. A modest high school goes for $9 million, a small grade school, around $600,000. A library to serve a 45,000 person town takes about $1.7 million. A sewer plant to serve 1,000 homes will cost around $700,000.

For example, the city of Irvine has a Facilities Funding Task Force which inventoried the major facilities needed to serve new

Reprinted with permission from *Paying the Piper: New Ways to Pay for Public Infrastructure in California* (Sacramento: Office of Planning and Research, 1982). Project manager and editor was Dean Misczynski development.[1] Admittedly their tastes were a little refined, since they included a civic center, a performing arts center, and an additional library on their list of needs. But mostly they listed things like arterial and local streets, neighborhood parks, a school, and flood control arrangements. The costs they estimated were impressive: for each 1,000 residents, about 35 acres of land and $5.9 to $8.5 million in construction costs would be required for the facilities. These costs average $16,500 to $23,800 per house.

The arrangements used to pay for these things are undergoing an evolutionary spurt in California, for several reasons. Proposition 13 was most decisive. Before, property taxes paid by new residents helped pay for all this public paraphernalia, helped along sometimes by contributions from the well-filled local treasury. But since Proposition 13, new residents pay fewer taxes than they used to pay. By most accounts, the taxes aren't enough to cover all the costs[2] and local treasuries are comparatively bare.

State cutbacks have made it all worse. For example, state bond money used to be available to pay for school construction. Although the voters recently approved the first new school construction bond issue since Proposition 13, the money will only take care of part of the problem. Important federal money is also disappearing. The federal government paid 75 percent of the cost of virtually all sewage treatment plants in California for years; but that program is almost dried up now.

Local governments have options for paying for the facilities required by new development. If they have excess capacity in their sewer systems and schools, for example, they can simply absorb new development for a while. Many local governments in California have done that for the last couple of years. Especially since there has not been very much development for that time, this worked. But the slack will pull taut eventually, and is already doing so in many parts of the state. The San Jose area is almost out of sewer capacity, parts of San Bernardino County need new schools, some of Orange County has arterial streets jammed tight. New developments south of Sacramento need schools, fire stations, and other facilities that no one is anxious to pay for.

Local governments that need new public structures can also absorb, in the sense of paying for those structures out of existing revenues. Some jurisdictions will do that. But probably not many. For one thing, there just is not enough money around. For another, new growth is not so overwhelmingly popular in many areas that citizens are anxious to see *their* taxes used to build things to serve *new* residents. Even if officials feel some sense of responsibility to help new housing along, the politics of doing so can be tough if the voters feel this way.

It is when local officials decide they need to raise new money to pay for these facilities that most of the evolution is taking place. There are two branches. One involves levying new taxes on the entire community and using the money to build new public facilities that will serve newly developing areas, although the money may well be used for other things as well. The other is to impose new taxes, charges, fees, or other levies that are more or less confined to the landowners, developers, or homebuyers of newly developing areas.

Until recently, it did not look as though there was much chance of levying new community-wide taxes for any purposes, let alone for new development facilities. As a practical, politically realistic matter, that is probably still true in most of California. Elected officials proposing new taxes are likely to be an endangered species in most of these parts. Nevertheless, recently the state supreme court glibly discovered that local governments have authority that hardly anyone suspected existed to levy new taxes. The court found that Proposition 13 does not prevent a local government from levying virtually any nonproperty tax if the revenues go into the general fund, so long as the local government can find authority somewhere to levy the tax.[3] They found that special districts which did not have authority to levy property taxes are not really special districts within the meaning of Proposition 13, and therefore can levy nonproperty taxes even if the money goes into a special fund.[4] And they concluded that local governments can even levy property taxes in excess of 1 percent of market value if the money does go into the local pension fund.[5] These discoveries threaten to provoke a new, tighter, clean-up initiative to trail Proposition 13.

Despite all this newly discovered fiscal freedom, most local governments are likely to find it politically difficult (and perhaps philosophically undesirable as well) to levy broad new taxes that fatten the local exchequer sufficiently to allow much new spending on public capital facilities to serve new development.

Which brings us to the second evolutionary branch: levies contrived to make development pay for its own facilities. There is nothing new about this approach. It has long been standard practice to require developers to build many public facilities to serve their projects and contribute money to help pay for other public items. Current law clearly authorizes this sort of thing. For example, the California Revenue Bond Law of 1941 allows local governments to sell bonds to finance construction of a sewage treatment plant, and to collect monthly sewer charges and hook-up charges to pay off the bonds.[6] Alternatively, a special assessment could be levied to do the same thing. Similarly, there is nothing difficult about finding a way to finance a water supply system, a storm drain, a residential street, or a string of street lights. Existing law provides ample, well trodden ways to raise money for these things. Local officials and bond people have experience with them. If done carefully, they are legally bombproof. They work, predictably, unequivocally, and reasonably efficiently. The only evolution with these easy-to-finance facilities has to do with getting around rubs like voting requirements and interest rate limits.

Fiscal evolution is most active where existing law has gaps. It is difficult, under current financing law, to raise money to pay for facilities with two characteristics: (a) they don't produce revenue, and can't easily be made to (for example, sewers are easy because it is time-honored to charge a monthly sewer fee; police stations are hard because charging for a police call would invite riot); and (b) they serve an area larger than all but the largest subdivisions. The most important examples of hard-to-pay-for facilities are elementary and high schools,[7] police stations, fire stations, libraries, recreational centers, and sometimes parks. It is also difficult to come up with new money to maintain these kinds of facilities, and to operate them.

Who should pay?

Before proceeding to more technical talk about specific money raising methods, consider policy. Who *should* pay for public facilities needed to serve new development? This is a touchy issue, one of those seemingly esoteric things that people get heated about. It has no ultimately true answers, only values and opinions.

History gives perspective. The currently dominant methods used to finance public facilities in California have mostly evolved since World War II. The drift has been that local governments have gradually found more and more ways to get developers, landowners, and homebuyers to pay for their own facilities. Great inventiveness has produced a considerable choice of ways to squeeze facility money out of these turnips. Local governments charged more and higher fees for zoning changes, building permits, and water and sewer hook-ups and for monthly service. They imposed more subdivision exactions, requiring that developers "contribute" streets, sidewalks, street lights, sewers, storm drains, and eventually parks and temporary school buildings before they were given permission to subdivide. Cities invented the community development charge, the price a developer had to pay to "buy in" to a community. Counties created county service areas. Leasebacks, environmental quality act exactions, and development agreements were all used in part for the same purpose: making development pay for itself.

The result of this evolution can be summarized numerically. So-called cost/revenue studies have been popular in California for several years. They attempt to quantify all the costs of providing public services to a development, and all the public revenues that will result from the project, including such as the property tax, the sales tax, alcoholic beverage tax, vehicle registration, and transfer taxes. These studies represent an imprecise art which is best taken with some skepticism, because they are based on data which is often crude, and they are sometimes subject to crass manipulation. Nonetheless, the consensus view of the conclusions of most of these studies in the period before Proposition 13 was that new development more or less paid its own way. Some projects turned surpluses, some were fiscal losers, but on balance it was a wash.

Proposition 13 initially changed that. It removed a big piece of the property tax that used to roll into local coffers from new developments. It is simple to get a rough idea of the magnitude of the loss. Before Proposition 13, the owner of a new $100,000 house would have paid roughly $3,000 per year in property taxes, since the statewide average property tax rate was around 3 percent of market value. After Proposition 13, the tax was limited to 1 percent of value, so the owner paid only $1,000 per year in property taxes. The local government got $2,000 per year less. Over a reasonable 10-year financial planning period, the local government got $20,000 less in property tax revenues than it would have had (ignoring, for simplicity, discounting and appraisal peculiarities).

With this history, it seems fair to characterize current local government efforts to find new sources of money for public facilities as a search for ways to get new development to again pay for itself, as it did until Proposition 13 passed.

History aside, several complaints are regularly made against new arrangements that require developers, homebuyers, or landowners to pay for new public facilities. Most of these complaints fall into three categories.

Complaint 1   The first complaint is that all charges, taxes, fees, and exactions on development simply get added on to the selling price of the house. Since housing costs are already too high, adding on more charges is bad public policy.

Almost all economists agree that this argument is overstated and misused. They agree that a good portion of these various levies probably are passed on to owners of raw land in the form of lower land prices. Although the argument can be put vastly more technically, the simple version is this. A developer typically begins a project by doing a market survey to determine what price he can get for a given house in a given location. Suppose he finds that he can sell the house for $100,000. He knows that he can build the house for $80,000, including a reasonable profit. That means he can afford to pay $20,000 for land. If he has to pay more than that, he would lose money on the deal, and he won't go ahead. Now suppose the city levies a new $5,000 building permit fee. The fee doesn't affect the price the developer can get for his house: it's still set by the areawide market at $100,000. If he tries charging $105,000 for it, it won't sell. Indeed, if he could have sold it for $105,000 he would have charged that price in the first place, unless he was afflicted with unusual and unbusinesslike generosity. With the new fee, it costs him $85,000 to build the house. So he can only afford to pay $15,000 for the land. Over time, land prices can be expected to adjust accordingly. In this way the owner of the undeveloped land ends up "paying" the new levy. Of course, if the developer already owned the land when the levy was imposed, he may be the one stung.

This rather technical matter of who really pays a development levy is important. If these levies were really passed on to homebuyers, then it would be sensible to be cautious about them. If they are indeed passed back to landowners, then it is somehow less troublesome.

Unfortunately, there is no respectable empirical analysis about the way that increased fees affect housing prices. Partially, this vacuum exists because it is technically very difficult to separate out the effect of a fee increase from all the other factors that affect real estate values.

Complaint 2   The second complaint is that levies that require new development to pay for its own facilities are a kind of double taxation. The developer or homebuyer must pay general property and sales taxes, which go into the city's general fund and are used to keep the entire city going and in addition must pay special charges to build their own infrastructure. Newcomers end up paying twice as much as oldcomers for the same services.

The argument presumes that it is outrageous that new residents should pay two taxes rather than one, and more money overall than old residents. Perhaps it is. But another perspective should be kept in mind. General opinion and numerous studies support the view that new development costs local governments more to serve than it pays in taxes. If that is true, then taxpayers in the already developed part of town subsidize new development anyway, even if the new taxpayers do pay substantially more than the old taxpayers. From this point of view, it does not seem unreasonable for residents of the existing town to look for ways to reduce their subsidy of new development.

Why is it that residents in an older area can keep themselves going with a given property and sales tax, while a new area might be a net loser with the same taxes, especially since the new homes are probably more expensive and therefore draw even more property taxes? There are several answers. Most importantly, the public facilities in the older area are already in and largely paid for; they were built when things were cheaper and were paid for when the property tax was much higher than now.

Excess is possible. With imagination, it is clearly possible to load so many new charges onto a new development that it would pay its way and then some. In that case, complaint two is compelling.

Complaint 3   The third complaint is that these new levies constitute an ungenerous changing of the rules. Since time immemorial, the established community has subsidized the public service needs of newly developing areas. But now that the existing residents are there, they want to draw up the fiscal gangplank and not extend to newcomers the fiscal support that they themselves enjoyed.

There are two problems with this argument. First, there isn't any compelling evidence that the existing community ever did subsidize new development. The pre–Proposition 13 cost/revenue studies are inconclusive, but suggest that there wasn't much if any subsidy overall. Second, even if there was a subsidy, Proposition 13 increased it substantially. It is not necessarily ungenerous for existing residents to try to bring any such subsidy down to what it was before.

None of these arguments seems terribly convincing one way or the other. The most decisive argument is probably a more practical one. New development does need new facilities. There is little money in local government general funds to pay for it, and not much interest on the part of existing residents to tax themselves to pay for it. The state and federal governments are unlikely candidates for generosity at the moment, either. So at least for the time being, the *only* source of money for the facilities is likely to be the new development itself.

1. Irvine Facilities Funding Task Force, *Harvard Avenue Facilities Funding Task Force Report* (Nov. 1981).
2. Office of Planning and Research, *New Housing: Paying Its Way?* (1979).
3. *City and County of San Francisco* v. *Farrell* (1982) 32 Cal.3d 47.
4. *Los Angeles Transportation Commission* v. *Richmond* (1982) 31 Cal.3d 197.
5. *Carmen* v. *Alvord* (1982) 31 Cal.3d 318.
6. Government Code section 54300 et seq.
7. The newly authorized school bond will provide a temporary respite for schools, if and when the bonds are actually sold. But the $500 million bond issue faces an $800 million current estimated "need," and as state population increases, so will "need."

Selling Public Property: How To Do It Right

Bruce J. Bergman

Municipalities are becoming increasingly vigorous in selling off excess real property—and for good reason. Parcels and buildings lying fallow generate no taxes and cannot contribute to business growth or residential development. Moreover, the sale of property generates an instant infusion of cash for the public coffers.

Sometimes as vital as the sale of public lands and buildings must be approached with requisite care and foresight. It is not simply a matter of gathering properties and getting the best price for them. Consideration must be given to the objectives of the sale, how it is to be sold, for what price, under what financial terms, and with what conditions, if any, to be imposed.

Objective: pure sale vs. planning

A large vacant tract in an area zoned for apartment buildings would undoubtedly bring a handsome price for multiple dwelling or condominium construction. But if the municipality's water and sanitary facilities are so strained that such construction would require building a new water treatment plant, the monetary gain of a big sale price would be illusory.

Any sale of municipal property should be approached with a view toward planning. Some counties are too large to use property sales as a planning device, while others have the staff but don't consider the point, emphasizing only the monetary considerations. Both price and planning should be considered where possible to maximize each benefit.

Reprinted with permission from the September 1985 issue of *Public Management* magazine, published by the International City Management Association.

Method: auction or private sale

Local law may control certain methods of sale. Properties taken back for taxes must be auctioned, while those previously used for municipal purposes can be sold privately. (Or the reverse may be true, and there are any number of permutations of this concept.) Sometimes the law provides that all municipal property must be auctioned and only if the upset price is not achieved may there be a negotiated sale.

When a negotiated or private sale is authorized, the officials may nevertheless elect to go to auction. The reason is that a private sale is much more vulnerable to public attack, whether real or imagined. Since claims of favoritism may cast a pall upon such sales, the entire process could benefit by the auction route.

Another alternative is to advertise for proposals, with notices in appropriate papers inviting offers from parties interested in purchasing and developing certain parcels.

Price and strategy

Since local law may dictate a procedure to determine selling price, statute must be consulted. For example, there may be a provision that property taken for taxes must be sold for at least the amount of past due taxes.

But even if there are no statutory constraints, there are common sense approaches. Whether sale is to be by auction or negotiated contract, there should be some rationality behind setting an upset price. Using the tax parcel as an example, if the municipality took title for failure to pay $25,000 in taxes, that is a good starting point.

Suppose, however, that this is an apparently choice parcel that an appraisal reveals is worth $75,000. Should the guideline be just the past due $25,000, or is the $75,000 more realistic? Starting bids at the lower figure (or negotiating at that amount) should ensure a quick sale. That is perhaps an advantage, but one that may not yield the highest monetary return.

Yet, that still may be appropriate if it is the only way to induce purchase by a favorable developer. Assume by way of example that company X can put up two three-family homes in a certain area on that vacant parcel. The municipality very much wants that done. Company X will do so only if it must pay no more than $25,000. No one else even hints that they would erect the desired buildings. Under those circumstances, the seemingly deficient $25,000 price may on balance be the best deal.

Still further, starting at $75,000 means the purchaser is probably paying retail. Since buyers from municipalities usually expect a bargain, this posture may discourage any sale.

Of course, consideration of the views of the citizenry must be evaluated. Selling land "worth" $75,000 for only $25,000 may appear to be ill-motivated. The best intentions in the world may not be worth the loss of confidence in government that could be engendered.

On the other hand, that $75,000 may yet make more sense if the parcel is unique or if a particular developer has a special project designed for that one price.

Similarly, a vacant parcel providing a water view to a substantial abutting home may well be worth retail price—or more—to the homeowner who will pay anything to avoid construction tending to diminish the value or enjoyment of his property.

So, price really depends upon a myriad of factors varying too diversely to set a rule. At the very least, appraisals should be obtained so an area of price latitude can be determined. Then, all the cited factors can be weighed to arrive at the best course of action.

Municipal financing

There are three basic ways to finance the sale:

Private mortgage   As it is when one buys a house, a purchaser of municipal property could approach a bank or some other lender to get a mortgage. Except for major developments, the problem is that the purchaser doesn't want to bind himself to buy unless he knows for sure he has the mortgage. You don't want to grant the time it takes him to get the mortgage, since you don't know if there is a sale until the commitment is firm. This is therefore not the most common method to finance the sale.

Installment sale contract   Called in some localities the "deed in trust" or "trust deed," this is probably the usual way to finance when all cash is not demanded.

The purchaser makes periodic payments for a set number of years. At the conclusion of that time, the deed is delivered. Until all payments are made, the seller is the record owner of the property, with the purchaser having what is known as "equitable title."

If a default occurs, the city or county retains the payments to date. Taxes are usually to be paid, even though the purchaser does not have record title. There is great safety to the seller and pressure on the purchaser to complete the sale.

The difficulty is that it imposes impediments to future financing by the purchaser and is unsatisfactory in many respects because that purchaser is not the owner of record.

Municipal mortgage   In order for the city or county to take back a mortgage—thus becoming the "bank"—it must have legal authority to do so, which is not always the case. Even where such authority is found, some municipalities believe they lack the staff or expertise to be in the banking business.

Still further, other municipalities fear that, in the event of a default, they would be mired in foreclosure litigation. Although beyond the scope of this article, municipal mortgages can be a most effective financing device. If the property is worth reasonably more than the mortgage, the chance of failing to recoup the financed amount in the foreclosure is quite slim. Under proper circumstances, legal fees and costs are recoverable to the foreclosing party. When the mortgaged building is in physical jeopardy during the course of a protracted foreclosure, a receiver may be appointed to collect the rents and profits for the benefit of the lender.

Sale conditions

How does the seller ensure that the purchaser will comply with the terms of sale? One way is to put a restrictive covenant in the deed. To the extent these are valid and binding in your area—and the municipal legal officer must be consulted—a later breach of the covenant would allow the city or county to sue the owner to demolish an offending structure.

Another possible solution is to put a right of reverter clause in the deed, which says that a violation of the covenant will cause title to revert back to the city or county. Although not often used, and perhaps more difficult to enforce, such a clause is a possibility.

These safeguards, among others, are also applicable to negotiated sales where the contract of sale will itself recite the various covenants to be inserted in the deed. Here, too, there is room for additional protection. Consider these possibilities for the contract.

Nonassignability   Negotiation with a reputable builder who plans to erect luxury condominiums sounds like a good idea because you have faith in his experience and ability to do the job. But he may decide to turn over a quick profit and sell the land to someone else—a person in whom you have either no knowledge or little faith. All the restrictive covenants in the world give you only a right to sue. So, prohibiting assignment of the contract gives a better chance of completion by the party you prefer.

Time limitations   Particularly for major projects, the purchaser will insist that the closing of title be conditioned upon his obtaining financing. The time given to the developer is critical. It must be sufficient to allow him to get the commitment (perhaps 30 to 90 or 120 days). But a more extended time means essentially that you sold an option and just gave someone a chance to "peddle a deal." Moreover, your property sits useless and off the tax rolls during that period. Careful attention to this detail is required.

Taxes until closing   Sometimes financing may be so complex that you must give more time than you would otherwise prefer. Then, too, the prospective use may require approval of your zoning board or planning commission, which can be quite time-consuming. In addition, these steps might piggyback, so that zoning approval would have to be completed before an application for financing could be filed—or vice versa. It might not be unusual, therefore, to find the time between contract and closing stretching to a year or two.

During all this time the land remains unused and generates no taxes. Hence, it is a good idea to consider requesting some payment in lieu of taxes to begin after some reasonable time has expired.

Time to build   For any number of reasons too detailed to review here, a builder may wish to delay construction even after having received financing commitments and zoning approval. While title may have passed, your goal was to have something built—not just to have received the money. Therefore, consideration should be given to requiring construction to commence a certain number of days or months after various contingencies have been fulfilled, and to be completed within a set period of time. This helps ensure completion when you want it.

Interest on down payment   In many nongovernmental real estate transactions, the usual 10 percent contract deposit (often called "earnest money") either is deposited in a non-interest-bearing account or earns interest for the purchaser's account. Especially when the municipality is giving the purchaser broad time limits to fulfill contingencies, it may be wise to protect the taxpayers by having the down payment earn nonrefundable interest to the city or county if the transaction falls through. If the interest is not to your credit, you have given away what was in essence a free option.

For Further Reference

Advisory Commission on Intergovernmental Relations. *Intergovernmental Service Arrangements for Delivering Local Public Services: Update 1983.* Washington, D.C., October 1985.

———. *The States and Distressed Communities: The Final Report.* Washington, D.C., November 1985.

Alonso, William. "Predicting Best with Imperfect Data." *Journal of the American Institute of Planners* 34, no. 3 (July 1968): 248–55.

American Planning Association. *Local Capital Improvements and Development Management: Analysis and Case Studies.* Chicago, 1980.

Aronson, J. Richard, and John L. Hilley. *Financing State and Local Governments,* 4th ed. Washington, D.C.: Brookings Institution, 1986.

Ascher, William. *Forecasting: An Appraisal for Policy Makers and Planners.* Baltimore: Johns Hopkins University Press, 1978.

Atkinson, Jeff. "User Fees: The Next Move." *American City & County* 100, no. 6 (June 1985): 54–60.

Bahl, Roy. *Financing State and Local Government in the 1980s.* New York: Oxford University Press, 1984.

Bahl, Roy, and Larry Schroeder. "Forecasting Local Government Budgets." Occasional Paper No. 38, Metropolitan Studies Program, Maxwell School. Syracuse, N.Y.: Syracuse University, 1979.

Benest, Frank. "Removing the Barriers to the New Entrepreneurship in City Government." *Western City* 61, no. 2 (February 1985): 13–14.

Berger, Peter L., and Richard John Neuhaus. *To Empower People.* Washington, D.C.: American Enterprise Institute, 1977.

Berger, Renee A., and Diane Rooney. "Public/Private Partnerships Thrive in Small Cities." *Public Management* 67, no. 12 (December 1985): 6–7.

Bierman, Harold, Jr., and Seymour Smidt. *The Capital Budgeting Decision.* New York: Macmillan, 1980.

Bozeman, J. Lisle. "The Capital Budget: History and Future Directions." *Public Budgeting & Finance* 4, no. 3 (Autumn 1984): 18–30.

Bretschneider, Stuart, and Larry Schroeder. "Revenue Forecasting, Budget Setting and Risk." *Socio-Economic Planning Science* 19, no. 6 (1985): 431–39.

Burchell, Robert W. *The New Reality of Municipal Finance.* New Brunswick, N.J.: Rutgers University, 1984.

California Office of Planning and Research. *Economic Practices Manual.* Sacramento: State of California, 1984.

Campbell, Candace. "Business Incubators: Creating Hatcheries for New Business, Jobs." *Western City* 61, no. 4 (April 1985): 3.

Carroll, John, Mark Hyde, and William Hudson. "Economic Development Policy: Why Rhode Islanders Rejected the Greenhouse Compact." *State Government* 58, no. 3 (Fall 1985): 111-12.

Chang, S. "Municipal Revenue Forecasting." *Growth and Change* 10, no. 4 (October 1979): 38-46.

Chapman, Jeffrey I. "An Economic Analysis of Some Local Responses to Fiscal Stress." *Policy Studies Review* 3, 1 (August 1983): 85-89.

────. *Changing Patterns of Land Use Regulation: Interaction Between Regulatory Policy and Public Revenues*. Report to the National Science Foundation, Grant Number SES-8218812, October 1984.

────. "Fiscal Stress and Budgetary Activity." *Public Budgeting & Finance* 2, no. 2 (Summer 1982): 83-87.

Chapman, Ronald. "Capital Financing: Time for a New Look at an Old Idea." *American City & County* 98, no. 6 (June 1983): 55-57.

Choate, Pat, and Susan Walters. *America In Ruins: Beyond the Public Works Porkbarrel*. Washington, D.C.: Council of State Planning Agencies, 1981.

Dowell, David E. "Applying Real Estate Financial Analysis to Planning and Development Control." *Journal of the American Planning Association* 51, no. 1 (Winter 1985): 84-94.

Ferris, James, and Elizabeth Graddy. "Contracting Out: For What? With Whom?" *Public Administration Review* 46, no. 4 (July/August 1986): 332-44.

Gabriel, Stuart, Lawrence Katz, and Jennifer Wolch. "Local Land-Use Regulation and Proposition 13." *Taxing and Spending*, Spring 1980, pp. 73-81.

Goldman, Harvey, and Sandra Mokuvos, "Local Government Financing: The Shirttails or the Alternatives?" *American City & County* 99, no. 3 (March 1984): 30-36.

Gordon, Janet R. "Banks and Small Business Development." *Public Management* 67, no. 12 (December 1985): 11-12.

Gregerman, Alan S. "Building an Effective Enterprise Development Strategy." *Public Management* 67, no. 12 (December 1985–): 8-10.

Harrison, Bennett, and Sandra Kanter, "The Political Economy of States' Job

Creation Business Incentives." *Journal of the American Institute of Planners* 44, no. 5 (October 1978): 424-35.

Holland, Stuart. *The State as Entrepreneur*. London: Weidenfeld and Nicolson, 1972.

Houck, Lewis Daniel, Jr. *A Practical Guide to Budgetary and Management Control Systems*. Lexington, Mass.: Lexington Books, 1979.

Humphrey, Nan, Mary John Miller, and Steve Godwin. "Revitalizing Greater Cleveland's Public Infrastructure." *Governmental Finance* 13, no. 3 (September 1984): 15.

Kets de Vries, Manfred F. R. "The Dark Side of Entrepreneurship." *Harvard Business Review* 63, no. 6 (November-December 1985): 160-67.

King, Norman. "The Economics of Demand Management." *Western City* 62, no. 10 (October 1982): 25-34.

Kirlin, John J. "Public Entrepreneurship." In *Committee on 21, 1986 Annual Report*, by John J. Kirlin. Sacramento, Calif.: League of California Cities, 1986.

Kirlin, John J., and Jeffrey I. Chapman. "Active Approaches to Local Government Revenue Generation." *The Urban Interest* 2, no. 2 (Fall 1980): 83-91.

Kirlin, John J., and Anne M. Kirlin. *Public Choices—Private Resources*. Sacramento, Calif.: California Tax Foundation, 1982.

Kolderie, Ted. "The Two Different Concepts of Privatization." *Public Administration Review* 46, no. 4 (July/August 1986): 285-91.

Ladd, Helen F., and T. Nicolaus Tideman. *Tax and Expenditure Limitations*. Washington, D.C.: Urban Institute, 1981.

League of California Cities. *Development Agreements*. Sacramento, Calif.: League of California Cities, 30 December 1980.

Leary, Thomas J. "Deindustrialization, Plant Closing Laws, and the States." *State Government* 58, no. 3 (Fall 1985): 113-18.

Markusen, Ann R. "High-Tech Jobs, Markets and Economic Development Prospects: Evidence from California." *Built Environment* 9, no. 1 (1983): 18-28.

McGrath, Dennis. "Who Must Leave?

Alternative Images of Urban Revitalization." *Journal of the American Planning Association* 48, no. 2 (Spring 1982): 196–203.

McPhail, Norman K. "5 Steps to Success in Municipal Financing." *Public Management* 67, no. 7 (July 1985): 21–23.

Misczynski, Dean. "The Fiscalization of Land Use." In *California Policy Choices*, vol. 3, edited by John J. Kirlin and Donald R. Winkler, 73–105. Los Angeles: University of Southern California, 1986.

Odell, Rice. "Can We Afford to Maintain Our Urban Infrastructure?" *Urban Land* 41 (January 1982): 1

Olstein, Myron, and Paula Stuart. "Financial Models as a Tool for Strategic Planning." *Government Finance Review* 1, no. 1 (April 1985): 12–17.

Pascal, Anthony, and Aaron Gurwitz. "Picking Winners: Industrial Strategies for Local Economic Development." Santa Monica, Calif.: Rand Corporation, 1983.

Peirce, Neal R., and Robert Guskind. "Fewer Federal Dollars Spurring Cities to Improve Management and Trim Costs." *National Journal*, 1 March 1986, 504–508.

Peiser, Richard B. "Does It Pay to Plan Suburban Growth?" *Journal of the American Planning Association* 50, no. 4 (Autumn 1984): 419–33.

Peiser, Richard B. "Financial Feasibility Models in New Town Development: Risk Evaluation in the United States." *Town Planning Review* 55, no. 1 (January 1984): 75–90.

Peltz, Michael, and Marc A. Weiss. "State and Local Government Roles in Industrial Innovation." *Journal of the American Planning Association* 50, no. 3 (Summer 1984): 279–79.

Petersen, John E., and Wesley C. Hough. *Creative Capital Financing for State and Local Governments.* Chicago: Government Finance Officers Association, 1983.

Poister, Theodore H. "A HUD Capacity Sharing Effort: The Financial Trend Monitoring System." *Public Budgeting & Finance* 6, no. 2 (Spring 1986): 20–32.

Public Technology, Inc. "Multi-Year Revenue and Expenditure Forecasting: Report of National Workshops." Washington, D.C., 1980.

Rose-Ackerman, Susan. "Beyond Tiebout: Modeling the Political Economy of Local Government." In *Local Provision of Public Services: The Tiebout Model after Twenty-Five Years*, edited by George R. Zodrow, 55–84. New York: Academic Press, 1983.

Rosenberg, Philip. "User Fee Establishment Depends on Community." *American City & County* 100, no. 6 (June 1985): 61–62.

Rubin, Irene S. *Running in the Red: Why Cities Go Broke*. Albany: State University of New York, 1982.

Schroeder, Larry. "Local Government Multi-Year Budgetary Forecasting: Some Administrative and Political Issues." *Public Administration Review* 42, no. 2 (March/April 1982): 121–27.

Seymour, Thomas J. "A Practical Approach to Business Retention." *Public Management* 67, no. 12 (December 1985): 17–18.

Siegel, Larry, and Ronald D. Doctor. "Privatizing Infrastructure May Prove Cost-Effective." *Western City* 61, no. 6 (June 1985): 7.

Smith, Janet Kiholm, and Richard L. Smith, III. "State and Local Fiscal Policy: Implications for Property Values and Economic Growth." *Public Finance Quarterly* 12, no. 1 (January 1984): 51–76.

Stanfield, Rochelle. "The Users May Have to Foot the Bill to Patch Crumbling Public Facilities." *National Journal*, 27 November 1982.

Sternlieb, George, and David Listokin. *New Tools for Economic Development: The Enterprise Zone, Development Bank, and RFC*. Piscataway, N.J.: Rutgers University, 1981.

U.S. Congress. Congressional Budget Office. *Public Works Infrastructure: Policy Considerations for the Future*. Washington, D.C.: Government Printing Office, April 1983.

————. Joint Committee on Taxation. *Summary of Conference Agreement on H.R. 3838 (Tax Reform Act of 1986)*. Washington, D.C.: Government Printing Office, 1986.

U.S. Department of Housing and Urban Development. *The Fiscal Impact Guidebook*. Washington, D.C.: Government Printing Office, 1980.

U.S. Department of Housing and Urban

Development. Office of Policy Development and Research. *Factors Related to Local Government Use of Performance Measurement.* Washington, D.C.: Government Printing Office, 1978.

Vaughn, Roger J. *Rebuilding America: Financing Public Works in the 1980s,* vol. 2. Washington D.C.: Council of State Planning Agencies, 1983.

Vincent, Phillip E. "Encouraging Economic Growth." In *California Policy Choices,* vol. 2, edited by John J. Kirlin and Donald R. Winkler, 63–93. Los Angeles: University of Southern California, 1985.

Vogt, A. John, and Lisa A. Cole, eds. *A Guide to Municipal Leasing.* Chicago: Government Finance Officers Association, 1983.

Wilson, B. Gale, and Donald D. Brown, "The Entrepreneurial Municipal Strategy." *Public Management* 65, no. 4 (April 1983): 10–13.

Zorn, C. Kurt. "Financing Infrastructure to Promote Economic Development in the East North Central Region." *Government Finance Review* 2, no. 2 (April 1986): 29–34.

Practical Management Series

**Long-Term Financial Planning:
Creative Strategies for Local Government**

Text type
Century Expanded

Composition
Unicorn Graphics
Washington, D.C.

Printing and binding
R.R. Donnelley & Sons Company

Cover design
Rebecca Geanaros